Psychology of a Medium

A Look at the Paranormal and the World of Mediums

Psychology
of a Medium

A Look at the Paranormal
and the World of Mediums

Billy Roberts

Winchester, UK
Washington, USA

First published by Sixth Books, 2012
Sixth Books is an imprint of John Hunt Publishing Ltd., Laurel House, Station Approach,
Alresford, Hants, SO24 9JH, UK
office1@jhpbooks.net
www.johnhuntpublishing.com
www.6th-books.com

For distributor details and how to order please visit the 'Ordering' section on our website.

Text copyright: Billy Roberts 2011

ISBN: 978 1 78099 396 6

A CIP catalogue record for this book is available from the British Library.

Design: Stuart Davies

Printed and bound in the USA by Edwards Brothers Malloy

We operate a distinctive and ethical publishing philosophy in all
areas of our business, from our global network of authors to
production and worldwide distribution.

CONTENTS

Introduction

The increase in the amount of paranormal television programs being broadcast today is no doubt the reason why the subject has become quite fashionable. In comparison to twenty-odd years ago mediums can now be found everywhere, and every theatre program contains at least one 'psychic' show per month. Mediums and followers of the paranormal might see this as progress where their profession is concerned, while the more serious devotee of the subject may well view it as retrograde step. Regardless of how you yourself view the paranormal, one cannot dispute the fact that it is a subject which today generates a great deal of revenue, and whether you are a tarot reader offering a 'one-to-one' service, or a stage medium/psychic touring the theatre circuit, the opportunities to make a lot of money are endless. Although I have been mediumistically inclined since I was very young (something that is always claimed by mediums, according to skeptics), I have always been quite radical in my approach to the subject, and have always maintained an extremely healthy skeptical attitude toward the paranormal as a whole. Given that I am a professional medium I know my claim of skepticism is somewhat paradoxical to say the least, but because I have found mediumistic skills to be the most unreliable of all paranormal abilities, I have always found it necessary to be extremely analytical about the way my skills work or do not work, whichever the case may be. Before I actually began to use my mediumistic abilities publically, I made it my business to see as many mediums and clairvoyants as I possibly could. Apart from attending public demonstrations of mediumship in Spiritualist Churches (and in occasional theatres) I also had private consultations with over 1000 mediums, the majority of whom came from different parts of the UK and sometimes overseas. As it is very rarely possible to recall everything that has transpired during a private consultation, I always recorded each session so that I could make a detailed study of them later. Although I had never doubted my own mediumistic skills, I needed to draw comparisons between my own abilities and the abilities of other mediums. This could only be successfully achieved by actually seeing as many mediums' work as I possibly could. I do have to say, although I was extremely fascinated with the whole subject matter, had it not been for my mother's and aunt's support and relentless encouragement, I am quite certain I would have become very disillusioned and quickly abandoned my quest. Needless to say, my interest in paranormal skills rapidly increased, and not only did I want to refine my own abilities, but I also wanted to know why and how they worked. Although I have had 16 books published on how best to develop your full psychic potential, I have now decided to explore the whole psychology of mediumship, how and why it works, and what makes individuals. I have always maintained that while everyone possesses psychic abilities potentially, mediumistic skills are completely different. In fact, mediums are born and not made, and one can only cultivate mediumistic skills when the potential is already present. And so, what is it that makes an individual with little or no mediumistic abilities actually believe that they do have the potential to work as a medium? One very important reason is the absence of legal or official monitoring of mediums and clairvoyants. No special credentials or qualifications are required for an individual to begin working as a medium or clairvoyant. In fact, it's not so much what you know as it is who you know in the mediumistic arena. In theory anyone gifted with a personality combined with oratory skills could set themselves up as a clairvoyant or medium. Even on the Spiritualist Church circuit, it is not all that difficult to infiltrate the very often closed mediumistic circles to be invited to give messages from the church platform. Although it has now been some years since I demonstrated my abilities in

Spiritualist Churches, before I began touring the theatre circuit I served my so-called mediumistic apprenticeship in Spiritualist Churches all over the UK and found these remarkably different to working in theatres. In fact, there is a marked difference in the psychology of Spiritualist Church mediums as opposed to mediums working in theatres. Giving so-called 'messages' to selected members of a theatre audience requires a completely different technique than is required to demonstrate mediumistic skills in a Spiritualist Church, and once a medium has embarked upon the theatre circuit he or she will find it extremely difficult to adjust to the Spiritualist environment. In my analysis of the psychology of a medium many things need to be considered. Is it normal to 'see' so-called 'dead' people? Are there any significant neurological changes in the brains of genuine mediums? What is it that transpires to make an individual actually want to be a medium? Are mediums self-deluded? These are just some of the questions I will endeavor to answer in the following pages, and although I am a professional medium, during my treatment of the subject I will play the 'devil's advocate' and do all in my power to answer the question, "Who is right, the skeptic or the medium?" To enable me to do this successfully, I must look at the vast subject of the paranormal from two very different perspectives.

Chapter One

Neurological Analysis

I am quite certain that most people would agree that the brain is an extremely complex organ, and also something of which a very small portion is used. But is a genuine medium really neurologically different to an ordinary person? Over the years there has been a great deal of research into the functioning of the brains of mediums and psychically inclined individuals, and the conclusions of the various researchers appear to have been unanimous. In America autopsies were actually carried out on the brains of deceased mediums, and it was found that the pineal glands in each were considerably larger than normal.

Russian Research

In 1903, Ivan Tutinsky, a Russian neuroscientist at Moscow University, became so interested in children with unusual paranormal abilities, that he compromised his professional integrity to make a study of them, and was thus ridiculed by his peers. Although Tutinsky took pains to avoid such terms as 'psychic' or 'paranormal', his seven-year research was fairly conclusive, inasmuch as he was fully convinced that he had discovered the cause of such supersensual abilities. In the first instance, Tutinsky concluded that the pineal gland of a child was much larger than that of an adult, and in the second instance, he discovered it was more developed in the female than in the male. Tutinsky was in no doubt that minute crystalline deposits found around the pineal gland were responsible for the production of electromagnetic waves and caused extra-electrical activity in the brain. This neurological phenomenon, he was certain, not only enabled the individual's brain to monitor molecular changes in the atmosphere, but also allowed it to receive information from the invisible universe, without the intermediary of the five ordinary senses. Although Tutinsky was initially considered somewhat a 'crank', his radical and very innovative research into extrasensory skills made him a pioneer in the field and eventually earned him the respect of his peers.

Since those early pioneering days great advancements have been made in Russia, America and Japan, with a constantly growing interest in metaphysics and all-things paranormal. Researchers into paranormal abilities have over the years concluded that there are marked neurological changes in the brains of those endeavoring to cultivate mediumistic abilities, and noticeable abnormalities in the electrical circuitry of the brains of those with well-established mediumistic skills. There is also some scientific evidence to suggest that significant changes occur in the nerve centers and that these changes somehow affect the hormonal system. Ivan Tutinsky believed that this was the very reason why women are often far more sensitive than men, and which is why they nearly always find it much easier than men to develop and cultivate extraordinary metaphysical abilities. As a consequence of this significant neurobiological phenomenon, researchers concluded that at least 70% of male mediums are gay or at least exhibit obvious feminine tendencies. This does not in any way suggest that cultivating mediumistic tendencies actually makes men gay, or that heterosexual men cannot be genuine mediums. On the contrary, the statistics previously given are merely the results of research carried out over the years, and it merely suggested that gay men as well as women do make far better mediums. In fact, endeavoring to cultivate the faculties, with the sole intention of developing mediumistic skills, somehow releases inherent feminine tendencies in some males.

But what is it about human nature that makes us so fascinated with the paranormal and particularly the unknown? When pushed, even the confirmed skeptic has a ghostly tale to tell. And so, it would seem that encounters with the supernatural are unavoidable, and regardless of what you say you do or do not believe, the paranormal is always an integral part of your life, even though you may not realize it. As long as it is healthy, I am most certainly all for skepticism. As far as I have always been concerned, it is always wise to question things, particularly those things for which conventional science does not have an answer. As I have already stated earlier, I have always been regarded as a 'skeptical' medium, and have always questioned my own abilities as well as the abilities of others. I have no doubt whatsoever that we live on in another dimension when we die, and that there is no such state as 'death'. In fact, there is only change, transmutation, growth, becoming a movement of matter or of consciousness from one condition to another. I am certain that nothing can ever die, and that it is possible for some 'gifted' individuals to receive communication from the inhabitants of those invisible dimensions. The only problems arise with the actual process of mediumistic communication, which is very often inconsistent and extremely unreliable. In fact, I would say that mediumistic communication is the most unreliable of all paranormal processes, and even when the medium is genuine and fully experienced the information produced is nearly always weak and ambiguous. I know this statement will anger or even offend many mediums, but this is just my personal opinion based primarily on my study of the subject, combined with the observations I have made over the last 30 years. During my studies of the mechanics of mediumship, I have found there to be significant trends and fashions in style and technique, particularly in the way different mediums work. In fact, in my experience very few mediums exhibit spontaneity and uniqueness, and the majority of them do make every effort to replicate the style and technique of the mediums they look up to and admire.

Seeing the Dead is Not Normal

Whichever way we choose to look at it, seeing so-called 'dead' people is certainly not normal and this phenomenon can sometimes have devastating psychological effects, particularly if the individual has a propensity towards nervousness and anxiety. Because very significant changes do occur in the brain and nerve plexuses during the process of psychic development, the aspirant should ideally be psychologically stable and fully aware of what he or she is actually doing. This might sound bizarrely far-fetched to those who are already working as mediums, and I can understand exactly why they may think that. However, having successfully run a center for psychic and spiritual studies for several years, I have witnessed firsthand what psychological damage can be sustained when one is completely ignorant of the implications of the process of psychic development. The majority of people interested in the subject approach it far too lightly, often without any consideration of the psychological and emotional changes that do occur during the whole process. During psychic development, a great deal of stress is placed upon the nervous system of the aspirant, and unless he or she is psychologically stable then all sorts of problems can occur. I am not simply making a wild statement for its effect; I am speaking purely from 30 years' experience of my involvement with the process of psychic development. And, believe me, the process of psychic development is a very precise science, and one which operates within its own laws. Any person seeking to cultivate the faculties with the sole intention of developing psychic or mediumistic abilities needs to be very disciplined and at all times mindful of what he or she is doing. The Law of Cause and Effect operates just as much in the mental world as much as it does in the physical and the moral worlds. Therefore, those seeking to develop their full psychic or mediumistic potential must take full responsibility for what he or she is doing, even when working under the supervision of an experienced teacher.

Chapter Two

Parapsychology and Skeptics

Today mediums and psychics working in the public arena require far more than an impressive ability if they are to stand up to critics and skeptics. They need to arm themselves with extensive knowledge of the paranormal and the way their ability actually works or does not work, whichever the case maybe. The growing interest in mediums and the paranormal has not only made the general public much more discerning where the process of mediumship is concerned, but now interest in the 100-year-old pseudoscience termed 'parapsychology' has increased, bringing the whole process of mediumship and the way it actually works much more under the analytical spotlight. There is only a small minority of the mediumistic profession who are able to argue in the defense of mediums, and although parapsychologists always appear to quote verbatim textbook research, primarily because of the majority of mediums' lack of knowledge, unfortunately they nearly always put forward an extremely good case. Unfortunately, the majority of mediums do not even bother to make a study of the way their skills actually work, and when confronted by parapsychologists and skeptics their ignorance always lets them down. I am not talking about self-confessed parapsychologists, but those who have graduated in psychology and studied parapsychology as an extra curriculum. These are a force to be reckoned with and the ones who are very often on a mission with nothing whatsoever to lose. As far as parapsychologists are concerned mediumistic skills are far easier to disprove than they are to prove, and to be quite honest, at the moment their assumption is correct.

Mediums are today in the proverbial spotlight, necessitating stricter laws and bringing the way they work more under the scrutinizing eye of parapsychologists and academic skeptics. While parapsychologists dismiss the information given by mediums to selected members of the audience as no more than 'cold reading', generalized and ambiguous messages that could apply to anyone, psychologist Paul Meehl referred to it as the 'Barnum Effect' after circus entrepreneur Phineas Taylor Barnum, a master psychological manipulator, who was known for his claim, "We have something for everyone!" A similar description of the information given by mediums is the 'Forer Effect', named after psychologist Bertram Forer who asserted that people who consult mediums and clairvoyants tend to accept vague and ambiguous statements as being personal to them, without actually realizing that the information they are accepting could really apply to anyone. In fact, parapsychologists appear to have a rational explanation for all alleged paranormal phenomena, attributing them all to either psychological or natural occurrences, or even chance and probability.

Parapsychology

Even the optical pastime many of us enjoyed as children, seeing anonymous faces in the patterns on curtains or the carpet, is dismissed by Klaus Conrad as no more than the psychological phenomenon, 'Apophenia', defined literally as seeing "patterns or connections in random or meaningless data". The majority of people have had the experience of thinking that they have heard someone call their name while taking a shower, even though there was nobody else in the house. Although quite spooky, parapsychology affirms that this is no more than the psychological phenomenon, 'Pareidolia', the auditory process involving the production of sounds and images in random stimuli. I am quite certain we have all experienced this phenomenon at some time or another. For example, the running water of the shower might give you the impression that the telephone is ringing, or you can hear disembodied voices having a conversation. Parapsychologists dismiss these sorts of phenomena as being all in the mind.

Paranormal investigators need to take care when involved in the Victorian pastime of so-called 'table-tipping'. According to parapsychologists, when the table rocks, or even when the pointer moves spontaneously across the Ouija board, this is the result of *Ideomotor Action*, involuntary muscle movements produced more by thought rather than by external stimuli.

Although parapsychology is the study of such paranormal phenomena as telepathy, telekinesis, mediumship, clairvoyance etc, it would appear that the majority of so-called high profile parapsychologists are only really interested in discrediting it and exposing all phenomena as 'fraud'. To my mind this is 'unhealthy' and not 'healthy' skepticism, and most certainly does absolutely nothing whatsoever for mediumship or the paranormal. I would agree that not all mediums are genuine, and that it is far too easy for anyone to begin working as a medium. However, to make such sweeping statements by dismissing it all as hokum is silly and not helpful where genuine research is concerned. When making a detailed analysis of mediumship, one also needs to explore the reasons why anyone would want to work as a medium in the public arena. Standing up before an audience is daunting enough, but when one is expected to deliver 'messages' to selected members of an audience, this is something completely different and places a great deal of stress on the medium. The question must be asked: is the stress greater for the genuine medium or the fake medium? Psychologically both are under a great deal of pressure, but although the genuine medium is psychologically prepared before going in front of an audience, it is not like being an actor, having to learn lines to play a particular character. It is more the medium who is not genuine who is very often prepared beforehand with various messages to pass on to selected members of an audience. These 'messages' most certainly DO fit the criteria of what has become fashionably known as 'cold reading'. Very often the unsuspecting recipient of the message is totally unaware that the information he or she is receiving from the alleged medium could very well apply to 90 percent of the audience. However, there are isolated incidents where the information given does not apply to anyone other than the individual to whom it is given. Still not a genuine message, this is termed a 'chance reading', and is a situation in which the 'medium' has simply been 'lucky'. This not only boosts the confidence of the message giver, but also impresses the audience, thus perpetuating the popularity of the medium. And so it goes on.

Mediums and Plants in the Audience

Skeptics, and some parapsychologists, frequently accuse 'stage' mediums of either having so-called 'plants' in the audience: individuals who pretend not to know the medium, and who will therefore acknowledge all the information given to them. And another suggestion is that the medium obtains prior information about selected members of the audience. I am not completely dismissing either possibility, but as someone who has been working in theatres for nearly 30 years I have to say that neither of these is a practical exercise. For one thing, involving other people in this sort of 'cheating' process would be extremely dangerous and the medium would always live in fear of being exposed. It's just not feasible, anymore than obtaining prior knowledge on selected members of the audience would be. If this were the case, mediums would produce remarkable results and would have hit after hit when delivering their messages. This suggestion is quite ridiculous! What next? Perhaps it will be suggested that mediums will have hidden UHF devices at theatres so that they can listen-in to audience conversations! I think not, what do you think? In saying this, since I started writing this book an extremely high profile television and stage medium has been accused of just that! It has been said that she had information relayed to her through an earpiece. Well, now I have heard it all! This really proves it: there is very little doubt that mediums are damned if they do and damned if they don't! They are criticized for producing astounding evidential messages, and ridiculed when they don't. Unfortunately, mediums are in a no-win situation, particularly in today's paranormal climate. Today it would seem that everybody is an expert; but mediums more than any other paranormal practitioners need to educate themselves in preparation for any confrontations that will at some point occur.

Chapter Three

Objective Reality and the Process of Communication

Einstein once posed the question, "Does the moon only exist when there is someone there to observe it?" Einstein made a valid point. He was a realist and believed that there was no such thing as an objective reality. This being the case then the mind – whatever the mind is – contains its own reality and also possesses a direct access to another dimension. Although now sounding very clichéd and steeped in fanciful New Age philosophy, this concept more or less concurs with the Buddhist description of Maya (illusion), the suggestion that the external world is unreal and transitory, and the only true reality lies within the innumerable dimensions of the mind. Then what of the soul after death? If nothing really exists outside of the mind, what *reality* does the soul or consciousness experience after death and what is it that mediums allegedly communicate with? As a medium myself, I know that such communication does take place, and that what transpires nearly always (not always as some communications are weak and ambiguous) proves the continuity of the soul beyond death. But how is this possible? Over the past 20 years I have gradually begun to question my own mediumistic skills, and in so doing have reached different conflicting conclusions. Apart from mediumistic abilities being the most unreliable of all paranormal skills, the information purporting to be from disembodied souls is very often quite inconsistent and way off the mark. One could say that this 'inconsistency' is down to lack of training on the medium's part, and that if the medium paid more attention to actually refining his or her abilities, the information produced would be more specific and far more accurate. Only the medium is qualified to assess the information he or she is receiving and to say whether it is coming from a discarnate source and not from their own *imagination*. When I first began working as a medium I was determined not to be like the majority of those I had seen demonstrating. I wanted to be specific and worked extremely hard at refining my skills. I had long since decided that if a medium could successfully give first names to a recipient, then there was no reason why the surname accompanied by road names and other details could also not be given! So, this brings me back to my first question: where does such information come from? Are we to believe that our deceased relatives and friends are at our beck and call all the time? If that is the case then what is the nature of life beyond death? Are we then to assume that death offers nothing more than an uneventful existence, and that the soul – whatever we conceive the soul to be – does not evolve, but remains for all eternity in a timeless, motionless void? This does not seem quite right to me, what do you think?

Multidimensional Universe

It is an axiom of physics that no two bodies of matter can occupy the same space at the same time; but millions upon millions of vibrations can exist in the one space without interfering with each other. The majority of esoteric and metaphysical traditions affirm that we do live in a multidimensional universe, in which there are worlds within worlds, each rising in a gradually ascending vibratory scale, from those which touch and blend with the highest planes of the physical world, to those which gradually merge with the lowest spheres of the great astral world. The majority of Eastern traditions all agree that nothing whatsoever can ever die! There is no actual state as death. There is only change, transmutation, growth, becoming a movement of matter or of consciousness from one condition to another. The human organism is far more than a biological unit consisting of a collection of cells. It is in fact an electromagnetic unit of incredible power, assimilating, transmuting and discharging energy, and is also contained within its own spectrum of light and color. Chemical energy undergoes a cellular process, thus converting it into light energy, culminating into what is known scientifically as bioluminescence, an optical phenomenon that is occasionally witnessed with some deep-sea aquatic creatures. Such energy is clearly an external manifestation of an internal process, and is therefore able to integrate with all other energies. Even at death such energy can never be lost, but merely transmutes into a different form, thus allowing it a continued existence in a different area of the universe. Even science informs us that there is actually no such state as death; as stated before, there is only change, transmutation and growth, becoming a movement of matter or consciousness from one condition to another. Even with this knowledge, the question must arise: "To where do we go when we die?" That is if we go anywhere at all! The whole psychology of mediumship is primarily based on communication received from a discarnate source. Whether such communication originates from a disembodied intelligent source, by means of the process of telepathy, or whether it originates from within the consciousness of the medium, is a question that really must be addressed. As a clairaudient/clairvoyant medium, I can only describe my own experience as the 'subjective processing' of external information. During the process of actually 'receiving' information, it sometimes feels like having a radio tuner inside my brain, and other times it feels like my consciousness is filtering extraneous thoughts, which then become a sequence of audible dialogues that I am then able to pass on to a selected member of the audience. I am only satisfied that it has originated from an external intelligent source once the information I have given has been acknowledged and thus confirmed. However, this is not always the case, and there are many occasions when the information is not accepted. In my younger years this apparent failure greatly concerned me, as this made me question the source of the information. As I developed an understanding of the way the whole communication actually worked, I began to realize that the fault did not lie with me alone.

Three-Way Communication

During the process of communication there are three intelligences involved: the medium, the disembodied soul, and the recipient of the information. In order to make the whole process work effectively total co-operation is required between all three parties. It is just as important to be a good recipient of a so-called 'message' as it is to be a good medium. If we accept that the third party involved in the process of communication is really a disembodied soul, then you must also understand that this energy source must also develop the ability to 'communicate' the information efficiently and with ease. This is not an excuse for the frequently witnessed poor quality of mediumship, but more to apportion the responsibility in the whole process of mediumistic communication. Mediums are very often lazy and do not make the effort to refine their skills and encourage the communicator to work harder and be more determined to establish a positive link. This is one of the many observations I have made over the years, and it was this that made me look more closely at my own mediumship. Whether we like it or not, the process of mediumship does not stand up to scrutiny, and it is this that causes mediums and clairvoyants to be ridiculed by skeptics and parapsychologists alike.

Mediums Are Born and Not Made

Although not very clear, there is a definite psychology behind mediumship and the whole process of mediumistic communication. I have always affirmed that 'mediums are born and not made' and I can never understand why anyone with no apparent mediumistic abilities would ever want to be a medium! Everyone possesses psychic abilities potentially, but I do believe that mediumistic skills are not as common and can only be developed in a much smaller minority than most people believe.

Whatever you think of mediums and clairvoyants, it is today extremely fashionable to be involved in some way with the paranormal. Today mediums and so-called 'Ghost Hunting' groups can be found everywhere, a clear indication that we have gone paranormal crazy. Make no mistake about it, there are definite psychological factors for a person wanting to be involved in the paranormal, and these nearly always fall outside of the parameters of mere healthy interest.

Chapter Four

Things That Go Bump in the Night

When is a haunted house not a haunted house? That is the question to which there is more than one answer. As I have already said in the previous chapter, today it is very fashionable to be involved in the paranormal. More than this though it is very often quite a lucrative profession to be involved in, if everything is done properly that is. Although there are no guarantees where paranormal phenomena is concerned, the devotees of the subject are still willing to pay the requested fee for an 'overnight stay' in an alleged haunted location, hoping that something of a paranormal nature will be experienced. More often than not, long before the paranormal enthusiast arrives at the location, his or her mind will have long since created its own ghosts and demons, and so by the time the so-called 'vigil' actually begins, the mind of the individual is already highly charged with 'orbs', shadowy apparitions and other supernatural anomalies. Because a house is purported to be 'haunted' does not in any way mean that paranormal phenomena is guaranteed. Paranormal fever is highly contagious and spreads very quickly through the shadows of an old manor house. In fact, what one person claims he or she has seen, another person will say that they have also seen, only more. It is human nature to embroider paranormal experiences, sometimes unintentionally. When you are in a highly charged situation where the hairs on the back of your neck are standing up, the brain is thrown into 'overdrive' and the mind does not have sufficient time to assess and calculate. This means that the imagination begins to create its own images, sensations and thoughts. These are swiftly passed on to the brain in quick succession, causing the 'paranormal terrors' to be triggered.

Paranormal phenomena can be quite spontaneous and may occur in the blinking of an eye. One of the most common paranormal occurrences is known as the so-called 'corner-of-the-eye' syndrome. These are images, such as shadowy forms or light anomalies, that appear in the peripheral sight. They usually quickly disappear when you turn your head to take a proper look at them. Whether there was anything really there in the first place is another question. Who can tell what happens when the imagination of the 'Ghost Hunter' is so highly charged?

Electromagnetic Unit

So, are all so-called apparitions the ghostly manifestations of discarnate spirits? Research carried out in Russia some years ago concluded that the human organism is not only an electromagnetic unit of incredible power, but that it also possesses a bioplasmic body – an energy vehicle that is able to integrate with and affect the surrounding environment. This would suggest then that families leave their individual imprints in the atmosphere of the house where they live, which may be experienced by future inhabitants. These imprints are synonymous with photographic images that can be 'replayed' for many years after, giving the impression to those who witness them that they have in actual fact seen a 'ghost'. Technically speaking they have seen a ghost, but not a conscious spirit with intelligence. This is usually referred to as 'environmental memory', the theory that every thought and action is locked in time and can thus be spontaneously accessed. A similar phenomenon is the 'stone tape' theory in which the bricks and mortar of a building retain sounds and feelings of all those who have lived there in the past. Just as audio and video tapes are coated with an electromagnetic substance, so too is there an electromagnetic energy field capable of 'capturing' past events and locking them in the stone structure of a building. These phantom images are periodically released to be witnessed by all those in close proximity, who usually announce that they have seen a ghost. I am not in any way suggesting that there is a rational explanation for all ghostly apparitions. On the contrary, this would only account for a minority of paranormal phenomena, and as a medium it would be silly for me to dismiss all phenomena as having an environmental or geological cause.

Geological Phenomenon

Triboluminescence is the geological phenomenon produced by friction of crystals or similar minerals below ground level. This phenomenon interrupts the electromagnetic field in close proximity resulting in some individuals having extrasensory experiences. One theory is that triboluminescence causes the electrical circuitry in the brains of highly sensitive individuals to be 'tripped', causing them to have hallucinations and to believe they have seen a 'ghost'. Individual who suffer from temporal lobe epilepsy are highly susceptible to triboluminescence and are likely to have transcendental experiences. Scientists have suggested that this is perhaps what happened to St. Paul when he experienced the blinding light on the road to Damascus. Theorists have suggested that St. Paul may have suffered from epilepsy, which would explain why he had the life-changing experience.

One thing is certain, once an individual has been bitten by the paranormal bug, it would seem that every commonplace phenomenon has a paranormal cause. Not everything that goes bump in the night is directly connected to disembodied beings, even if the phenomena have been produced by some sort of residual force. As far as I can see, the paranormal is an emotional as well as a psychological minefield, and this is no place for the fearful, faint-hearted or psychologically disturbed individual to be!

Although paranormal phenomena are exactly the same no matter where you are in the world, I have found that there are certain geographical locations in the world where the quality and consistency of it greatly differs. This statement may surprise the serious student of the paranormal, but when you have experienced being in the Louisiana swamps in the dead of night paranormal phenomena takes on a whole new meaning. In 2003, I was filming a documentary to promote Sony's PlayStation 2 game, *Ghosthunter*. Although we visited three haunted locations throughout New Orleans and the Gulf of Mexico, the haunted graveyard deep within the Louisiana swamps was by far the most interesting experience, as well as the most frightening. In the swamps we experienced all sorts of paranormal phenomena, from unexplained light anomalies moving through the uneven terrain, to ectoplasmic clouds forming unusual patterns in the eerie shadows cast by the moon. In all my years of paranormal research I can honestly say that I've never experienced anything like it before. As if that was not enough, we had to contend with the slithering snakes as we wended our way through the graveyard. Apart from all the visible phenomena, New Orleans parapsychologist Kalila Smith and I were both overwhelmed with a sense of foreboding. And to finish all this off, a large white owl hovered curiously above my head and remained there for at least ten seconds, an eternity when your whole body is trembling with fear.

Regardless of the depth of interest you have in the paranormal, it is important to keep your feet firmly on the ground, and question everything you and others experience.

Chapter Five

Science and the Paranormal

We are now living in an extremely exciting age of science and technology, where sophisticated scientific devices enable us to make a detailed analysis of paranormal phenomena when they occur. These devices allow paranormal investigators to approach the subject professionally and to be meticulous in their calculations and assessments. No self-respecting ghost hunter would be seen without an EMF Meter – an electromagnetic fluctuation meter to monitor fluctuations in the electromagnetic scale, helping the user to determine whether or not a discarnate being is responsible for the occurring paranormal activity. EMF Meters, infrared cameras, laser non-contact thermometers, night vision cameras and the very essential recording equipment are just some of the paranormal investigators' prerequisite apparatus. Of course, there are more sophisticated devices to help the serious student explore the world of the paranormal.

Kirlian Camera

In approximately 1939, Semyon and Valentina Kirlian, a husband and wife team from Krasnodar near the Black Sea, developed a crude photographic device to photograph auric energy radiating from the hands. The Kirlians believed that disease could be detected in the aura some time before it became apparent in the physical body, and this meant that the monochrome photograph could be used as a diagnostic tool. In fact, the Kirlians' innovative photographic device was an inspiration to many others working in the same field, and today a more sophisticated instamatic color camera is available, the photograph from which is accompanied by a full computerized detailed analysis of the individual to whom the auric image belongs. Although there has been some question as to whether or not the image captured by the camera is an accurate portrayal of the human energy field, the information produced by such cameras have caught the interest of scientists working in the field of energy. Experiments carried out with amputees proved fairly conclusively that the aura of the individual's leg was still very much apparent even though the leg had long since gone. The same experiment was carried out by photographing a leaf before and after it had been cut in half. The aura of the leaf was still intact even after it had been cut into two pieces.

Dr. Kilner and the Aura

In the early part of the twentieth century, Walter Kilner, a medical electrician from St Thomas' Hospital in London, developed what became known as a Kilner Screen. Kilner's simple device was comprised of two glass screens, in the center of which he poured a coal tar dye (dicyanin), a substance consisting of various degrees of an alcoholic solution. Kilner was extremely interested in metaphysics and, in particular, the human aura, and it was this interest that led him to conduct research into how he could make the aura visible to the naked eye. By standing the patient behind the screens, which he illuminated with an extremely bright light, he found he was able to actually 'see' the individual's aura. Kilner later published his findings in a book titled *The Human Atmosphere*, and which was later re-titled *The Aura*.

It is believed that the aura is caused by chemical energy being processed in the body's cellular structure, during which it is converted into light energy, culminating into what is known as human bioluminescence, an optical phenomenon which is occasionally seen with some aquatic creatures. It is now believed that the bioluminescence reveals disease and problems with the body's equilibrium. More recently scientists in Japan have used a cryogenic device to photograph varying degrees of color generated by heat in the physical body. This, they believe, is synonymous with the aura and can also be used to diagnose diseases.

Although the majority of people use the word 'aura' as a descriptive term, and say "He has an aura of peace," or "The house has an aura of warmth," we now know that the word aura is far more than a descriptive term. It is a scientific as well as a metaphysical fact, and over the years it has been the focus of a considerable amount of scientific research. Although the colors in the aura are known to change with every passing thought, feeling and emotion, as well as with the food we eat, there is also a predominant part of the aura that never changes. This represents the true character and nature of the individual, and it is this aspect of the human energy field that causes us to be repulsed or attracted to some individuals.

The Aura a Vaporous Mass

The aura has frequently been described as a vaporous mass of electromagnetic particles surrounding every living thing, and has historically been depicted in various ways. The halo of tradition painted by medieval artists around the heads of saints was in actual fact an integral part of the aura. The so-called 'halo' represented the individual's saintliness or divinity. Where medieval artists got the idea of the aura from in the first place nobody knows, but one thing is quite certain, they must have known about the aura to depict it in this way. The colored feathers in the headdress of the Native American chief also symbolized the aura. The many colored feathers represented his spirituality and status in the tribe. Even old sayings such as 'Yellow' when someone was a coward, 'Red with rage' and even 'Green with envy' are all references to the transitory colors in the aura. The human energy field is believed to be a sort of prehistoric radar device, more extensive at the back of a person than at the front, primarily to safeguard against predators. However, photographs of the aura of a visually handicapped person have revealed it to be just as extensive at the front as it is at the back, obviously to ensure that the person is able to negotiate his or her way unhindered by any obstacles.

Although the majority of people cannot actually see the human aura, the phenomenon is always sensed. When we find ourselves in an unfamiliar environment our aura expands protectively so that we can 'sense' approaching danger. We've all had the experience of sitting alone in a theatre, or even standing alone in a queue, when we feel compelled to look around to see someone staring intently at us. So, although the aura cannot be seen, it does have an extremely practical use, and is constantly scanning the surrounding environment for predators. Apart from being able to photograph the aura, using an extremely sophisticated energy-scanning device, its radiations can also be monitored and digitally observed. And so the aura is most definitely a scientifically proven fact!

Chapter Six

Mediums – Real or Not?

Primarily because of the attention mediums now receive on television today, the majority of those interested in the subject are more discerning and more likely to differentiate between a genuine and not so genuine medium. This is an extremely difficult subject, and because I am a medium, I suppose it leaves me wide open to criticism. Nonetheless, it is a subject I have always been passionate about and one that needs to be meticulously addressed in this book.

Scientific Testing

It is my personal opinion that while the skills of psychically inclined individuals can be scrutinized and tested under controlled laboratory conditions, because of its very nature, mediumship cannot! A psychically gifted person can be subjected to telepathic experiments, and even be given specific exercises to test their mental capacity, but mediumistic skills are controlled by completely different mental principles that will only function under certain environmental conditions. A medium's job is primarily to prove the soul's continued existence beyond death by giving detailed information about a person's deceased relatives or friends. Although mediums are frequently ridiculed and even condemned by the skeptically minded, psychically inclined individuals are not quite looked upon in the same way. Depending how impressive a psychic individual's abilities are, they are very often looked upon with awe. Mediums are not afforded the same credibility, and are nearly always dismissed without even little consideration. The psychology behind the attitude is fairly straightforward and very simple. Although a person may well believe in *life after death*, they may well have great difficulty in accepting that certain gifted individuals have the power to actually communicate with the so-called 'dead'! However, a skeptic's assessment of mediums as a whole is very often based on the fact that he or she may have seen one or maybe two mediums working, and whose abilities failed to impress. These facts being so then let's explore the way mediums actually work, not only from a skeptic's point of view, but also as a medium, from my point of view.

Mediums and the Barnum Effect

I mentioned in an earlier chapter that parapsychologists nearly always accuse mediums of using the Barnum Effect, ambiguous statements that could apply to anyone. So, what are they hearing mediums saying to make them accuse them in this way? Look at the dialogue issued in a typical 'cold reading' message below.

MEDIUM: *"I have a motherly figure here. She is saying that she misses and loves you so much, but wonders why you don't wear her ring?"*

MESSAGE RECIPIENT: *"I miss and love her, but I am wearing her ring."*

MEDIUM: *"I don't think she's referring to this ring. Wait a minute, I'll ask her. (Pauses) No, I thought not. She's talking about a ring set with a blue stone. She says it was surrounded by other smaller stones?"*

MESSAGE RECIPIENT: *"I'm not sure about that! I'd have to ask my sister."*

MEDIUM: *"She's concerned about a younger person. Do you have a daughter or a son?"*

MESSAGE RECIPIENT: *"One of each. But my daughter has had a few problems with a relationship."*

MEDIUM: *"Yes, that's right! She's saying she knows about it, and everything will be OK. She's not pregnant is she?"*

MESSAGE RECIPIENT: *"My god! I do hope not! She's only 16."*

MEDIUM: *"Your mother's saying it's not her. That's my fault, I'm sorry. But there is news of a baby coming soon – before the year comes to an end."*

MESSAGE RECIPIENT: *"Don't know who that could be! As long as it's not me!"*

And so the message goes on with the recipient occasionally leading or even feeding the medium. You will notice that not one name was given in this message, making it even more ambiguous. This may be a typically generalized message frequently given by mediums of a poor quality. Depending on the medium's personality, this sort of message frequently impresses those who have never seen a medium demonstrate before. From my point of view as well as a skeptic's, this message is poor, and as well as offering no evidence of survival, it most definitely could apply to almost anyone.

GENUINE MEDIUMISTIC MESSAGES

The content of the following dialogue taken from a mediumistic message is completely different, both in content and the way in which it is delivered. This cannot in anyway be considered ambiguous or generalized.

MEDIUM: *"I've got your father here, and he is with his brother James."*

MESSAGE RECIPIENT: *"Thank you. Yes, James was his brother."*

MEDIUM: *"Although they had always been very close, your father says that they fell out just before he died. This devastated James and he never really got over it. So, I'm presuming your father passed away before him! (Rhetorical.) Your father is showing me a leather pouch containing medals. One medal in particular has the name Peter Frederick Jones engraved on it. Do you understand this?"*

MESSAGE RECIPIENT: *"Yes, I do. Peter Frederick Jones was my* *father's name."*

MEDIUM: *"He is with his grandmother Florence, and her sister Barbara."*

MESSAGE RECIPIENT: *"Yes, his grandmother was called Florence, but Barbara was her eldest daughter."*

MEDIUM: *"I am sorry, that was my mistake. I don't know what St Michael meant to him, but I can see this written at the top of a letter."*

MESSAGE RECIPIENT: *"He and my mother lived at St Michael's Close."*

And so the accuracy of the message continues. This sort of message is obviously unique and could not apply to anyone other than the person to whom it is given. Even though this sort of information could not in any way be described as 'cold reading', skeptics and parapsychologists would still find something wrong in the content and the way the message was delivered. This proves once again that mediums are damned if they do, and most certainly damned if they don't!

Although some genuine mediums are capable of delivering messages far more accurate than the one given above, it must be said that it is a mediumistic process that cannot be executed all the time. I have already stated that mediumship is the most inconsistent of all paranormal abilities, and even the best of mediums do occasionally encounter difficulties, very often resulting from a poor or non-receptive audience.

Even the best and most accurate of mediums are criticized and condemned, very often anonymously on Internet blogs and forums. These attacks are frequently perpetrated by malicious individuals for no reason other than to inflict hurt and malign the name of the medium. This is another good reason mediums working on the circuit today should be thick-skinned and armed with knowledge of their craft.

As a medium myself it is expected that I defend all mediums.

However, it is because I do respect my profession and view the whole concept of mediumship extremely seriously that I can only defend what I feel are genuine mediums. Today it seems to be the general consensus of opinions that everyone possesses mediumistic skills potentially, at least to some greater or lesser degree. However, to reiterate what I have previously said, mediums are born and not made, and although everyone possesses psychic abilities potentially, mediumistic skills are only found in a minority of people.

Chapter Seven

Don't Shoot the Medium, He's Only the Messenger!

As a religion Spiritualism has indeed come a very long way in the last 50 years or so. In fact, it only became a recognized religion when an Act of Parliament made it so in 1952. Before that time Spiritualist meeting places would be held everywhere, from basements to a little room at the back of a shop on the high street. Even then it was nearly always viewed with some hilarity and cynicism, and whenever a group of girls were at a lose end and wanted somewhere to go for a night out, where better than 'the spooks', as it was frequently referred to. Today, although it is most certainly viewed with far more respect, Spiritualism is still greatly misunderstood by the majority of people, who expect the demonstrating medium to foretell their future, rather than pass on messages from their deceased relatives or friends.

The Church of England and the Majority Report

In 1937 Cosmo Lang, the then Archbishop of Canterbury, received many letters either supporting, or simply complaining about this 'unusual' religion, whose ministers (mediums) passed on messages from the so-called 'dead' to selected members of the audience. It is said that the Archbishop was so intrigued that he appointed a committee of ten signatories to investigate Spiritualism as well as the phenomena that was demonstrated within the confines of its churches. Even though the enquiry was completely impartial, the finished report did not come to light for some years, leaving Spiritualists all over the UK completely in the dark. A copy of the report (which was named the Majority Report) was somehow obtained by the editor of the Spiritualist paper, the *Psychic News*, ten years later, who published it in full. It was thought that the reason it wasn't made public in the first place was that the people who investigated Spiritualism were not against it, but totally in favor of it. In fact, the majority of the signatories were in agreement that if they were to dismiss the phenomena that were demonstrated in Spiritualist Churches, which was healing, clairvoyance etc, then one also had to dismiss the phenomena of the New Testament, which was in effect exactly the same. As a result of the report's publication a parliamentary act was passed and Spiritualism thus became a 'recognized' religion. Today Spiritualist Churches can be found all over the world, and unlike the orthodox churches, primarily because of the mediumistic demonstrations that take place during their services, Spiritualist congregations are on the increase. However, whether this would still be the case if the clairvoyant part of the services was actually stopped is a question that Spiritualists themselves ask. Nonetheless, it is still an extremely thriving religion that is growing in popularity by the year.

Spiritualism and Clairvoyance

Clairvoyance is to all intents and purposes an integral part of a Spiritualist service, and as soon as the hymn singing is over, one can rest assured that the congregation will begin to pay real attention, in the hope that the medium will come to them with a 'message'. Demonstrating mediumistic skills in a theater is completely different from working in a Spiritualist Church, simply because theater audiences pay for their tickets and really do expect something in return. Both theater audiences and Spiritualist Church congregations can be quite cruel, especially if they do not receive a message from the medium. In fact, it is only a very small minority of church congregations who just attend the 'service' simply out of loyalty and to support their church. I have known cases where a good medium has been condemned by some members of a church congregation, simply because they did not receive a message. The favorite complaint is very often, "My father has just died: I am sure he would have come to let me know he was all right! This medium is rubbish!" It sounds very childish, but I have seen it so many times. This would suggest then that as well as there being a very specific psychology of mediums and the way they work, there is also most definitely a psychology of those who go to see mediums; whether in a Spiritualist Church or a theater, it seems to matter very little. In fact, whether a medium is genuine or not, the psychology behind consulting mediums can sometimes work in his or her favor. For example, there are some individuals who consult their favorite medium on a fairly regular basis. "I feel comfortable with him/her and I wouldn't go to anyone else." This statement is quite common; and although the individual is no doubt loyal to their favorite medium, and goes to see them with all good intentions, they very little realize that the medium is bound to have accumulated knowledge over the period of time their 'client' has been to see them. By now they are on first-name terms, and the first thing that happens is the medium knows exactly what the client has come for. Retrospective analysis is the psychological process of retrieving information stored in the subconscious mind. Like anyone who works with people on a regular basis, mediums very often unconsciously develop retentive memories. Although the majority of mediumistic practitioners do work to a code of ethics with strict morals, there is a minority of unscrupulous mediums who do call upon the information they have already obtained in prior consultations. Occasionally the subconscious data about the 'client' is retrieved without realizing it, but very often the medium knows full well what he or she is doing. The client is usually oblivious to the dishonest practice and believes that their trusted favorite medium would never stoop to such levels of unscrupulous behavior. Occasionally the client may realize that the medium already knows the information which is being given during the consultation, but he or she is very often too polite to comment. Then there is the person who is clearly 'addicted' to clairvoyants and mediums and consults every practitioner she can. I say 'she' because it is mostly women, and men rarely make a habit of having lots of private consultations with clairvoyants, although I am sure there are exceptions. I am quite certain that being obsessive over anything can be emotionally damaging, and using clairvoyants and mediums to satisfy an obsession most definitely has its psychological implications.

I mentioned in an earlier part of the book that the amount of alleged mediums working today has increased greatly in comparison to 20 years ago. This clearly suggests that there is also an increase in interest in the paranormal, and is also an indication of just how easy it really is for a person to set themselves up as a medium or clairvoyant and begin working. A question I am frequently asked is, with so many mediums to chose, from how does one know who is genuine and who is not? This is a difficult question to answer, as you really have to see them before making a judgment. This practice can prove very costly and you may never really find a suitable medium or clairvoyant. My advice is to go by recommendation. Even though this is usually the best way to go about it, you may well find that what medium your friend finds suitable for her may well not be suitable for you. All mediums and clairvoyants are different, and one which suits one person most probably will not suit another.

Spirit Guides

It is all very comforting to know that you have a spirit guide guiding and watching over you, but unless you have actually witnessed it for yourself then it proves absolutely nothing whatsoever. Some mediums like to tell you about your spirit guide, but in my opinion it does not provide the evidence you should be seeking when consulting one. This sort of information is very often a good measure of a medium's ability, as many of them talk about spirit guides to 'fill-in' the time and get the private consultation over and done with! This is not to say that some mediums don't genuinely 'see' your spirit guide and simply feels the need to pass the information on to you because he or she feels it is important for you to know about it.

You may well have been so impressed with the accuracy of your first mediumistic consultation but totally disappointed with your second visit. As I have already said, mediumship is unreliable and inconsistent at the best of times, but when you have high expectations you can be greatly disappointed. The only people who seem to be able to guarantee a reading are the 'fake' clairvoyants. I am not talking about giving evidence of survival, but more telling you about your future. You need to be very selective when consulting a medium, and if you have suffered the loss of a loved one, do not consult a tarot reader or palmist. In saying this, primarily as a focal point and to look at your future and personal situations, many mediums do use tarot cards during the reading. Although I don't need them I do use them. Some people have difficulty in understanding how the information is obtained by a medium, and are very often comforted when they see some things like tarot cards or a crystal ball. Whoever you consult, all that is required from you is a simple "yes" or "no". Never lead the clairvoyant or fill in any blanks. It is sometimes necessary to answer "Yes, that's my mother," or whatever the case may be, but never offer any other information.

Whether you choose to accept it or not, not all mediums are genuine, and the onus is on you to complain well before your reading has reached it conclusion. You should have a pretty good idea after ten minutes whether or not you feel comfortable with what the medium or clairvoyant is saying to you. Listen carefully for the waffle, the useless time-wasting dialogue that the fake medium (and sometimes genuine) use to pass the time away and get the reading over as quickly as he or she can. Finally, once you have found a genuine and competent medium, and you are completely satisfied that he or she has proven to you that there is life after death, there should be no reason to see a medium again, unless of course you go to see one in a theater primarily for the enjoyment of it.

Chapter Eight

Genuine Versus Fake

In my experience and observations I have made of mediums over the last 30 years, it seems to me that the general public often confuse a good medium with a nice person. When demonstrating either in a theater or Spiritualist Church, there are prerequisites essential for a professional performance. Presentation and stage-craft are two things that help the medium take control of the audience, and as speaking is an integral part of a public demonstration, diction and oratory skills make the medium's performance appear professional and stand out above others. I have witnessed on so many occasions when the poor quality of an individual's mediumship has been masked by the fact that he or she was quite personable and had a pleasant manner. This personality type is in complete contrast to the arrogant medium whose attitude is rude and quite aggressive. The latter style of medium always fails to conceal their poor mediumistic skills, and his or her attitude never fails to alienate them from the audience thus inhibiting their performance. I have already established that the audience of a mediumistic or psychic show can be extremely cruel, and even when the medium's messages are extremely accurate, if there is no rapport between them and the audience, it will just not work, regardless of the quality of the medium's skill.

Although there are some excellent mediums around today, generally speaking the quality of the majority of mediums leaves an awful lot to be desired. Some mediums go through demonstration after demonstration without giving any names at all, while others give many first names, one after another, but no surnames.

Fake Mediumistic Skills Do Not Travel

While genuine mediums are able to work from one city to another, the not so genuine mediums have great difficulty when working beyond the confines of their own city. The primary reason for this is that names greatly change from city to city, and the fashionable names in the North of England will not be as common in the south. Social circumstances, work types and sometimes illnesses also differ from place to place, making it a little more difficult for messages to be placed. For example, my name, Billy, is not so typical in the South of England, or for that matter in any city beyond the North West of England. The generalized messages that will always be accepted by selected members of an audience in the North of England are very rarely accepted in the South of the country. This may sound difficult to believe, but I have made a detailed study of this phenomenon, particularly with the many mediums with whom I have worked over the years. And so you must be able to see that there is a psychology behind mediumship and the way it works or does not work. Unless the medium has genuinely received messages from a disembodied mind, then he or she would have great difficulty demonstrating to an audience outside of his or her own town. The process of mediumship is extremely stressful at the best of times, but 'faking' is most certainly more traumatic, both from an emotional and psychological point of view. Although there are exceptions to the rule (and this has been proven on numerous occasions), fraudulent mediums do not get away with it forever. There is an old and very meaningful saying, "You can fool some of the people some of the time, but you can't fool all the people all of the time." In saying this, one so-called 'high profile' medium has proven this wrong after his antics were exposed on national television. He went from strength to strength and is still as popular today as he was when he first graced our screens.

Fraudulent mediums have always been around, and many of those working in Victorian times were guilty of faking it.

Victorian Parlor Séance

The so-called parlor séance was the highlight of the week in the homes of wealthy people, when relatives and friends would be invited to sit round the table with the visiting medium, giving a whole new meaning to the statement, "Is there anybody there?" Occasionally there was somebody there; as a disembodied voice would boom through the aluminum trumpet, and those present watched in amazement as it rose spontaneously from the table to move quickly round the exuberant sitters who looked upon the eerie phenomenon in expectation. "Hello, my dear!" a voice would boom from the trumpet as it appeared suspended in mid-air, directly in front of one particular member of the circle. "It's your husband Alf!" Very often the whole procedure would appear quite genuine, but the majority of séance meetings were contrived with the fake medium being proficient in the art of so-called 'séance trickery', something that was extremely lucrative and common at the time. The Victorians were fascinated with the 'unknown', and even Queen Victoria consulted mediums to maintain her relationship with her deceased husband Albert. It is believed that her closest friend and servant John Brown was himself a trance medium, and it was he who allegedly brought mediums to see the Queen. Although the belief in an afterlife has been there from time immemorial, the Victorians were obsessed with it.

The Davenport Brothers

The Victorians' obsession with mediums and the afterlife gave rise to many charlatans, two of whom were the American Davenport brothers, Ira Erastas and William Henry. Their father was a Buffalo, New York policeman who became interested in the Fox sisters and the Hydesville Rappings. He formed a séance with his family, only to find that his daughter and two sons, William 14 and Ira 16, were mediumistically gifted. This was the beginning of the Davenport brothers mediumistic adventure.

They toured the world with their séance stage shows, astounding audiences everywhere with their astounding abilities. While appearing in France, Ira and William were summoned to give a demonstration of their skills before Napoleon and his wife. They too were absolutely amazed with the phenomena the Davenport brothers produced. They were allegedly the creators of the physical séance cabinet, used by many mediums even to this day. While spiritualists worldwide saw the cabinet as an innovation, skeptics viewed it suspiciously as a cunning way to conceal their trickery. As their popularity grew so did interest from skeptics, one of whom was the famous escapologist, Harry Houdini. It is said that the Davenports' demise came about when they appeared at St George's Hall in Liverpool, England. They asked if anyone from the audience would come on stage and secure their hands and feet with a knotted piece of cord. Unfortunately the Davenports picked on the wrong person. A Birkenhead dock worker secured them both with a 'fool's' knot, who knew full well that the only way they could free themselves would be by paranormal means. The audience watched in anticipation for the usual phenomena to occur. The Davenport brothers could not undo the dock worker's knots, and they were driven from the hall by an angry crowd, demanding their money back. Although the Davenports continued to perform before audiences worldwide, their popularity gradually diminished. Before William died he allegedly confessed that their shows had all been produced by the trickery of magic. The Davenport brothers' mediumistic abilities still remain a mystery today. Were they really gifted mediums who could produce such phenomena as musical instruments playing, as if by disembodied hands, levitation and other phenomena, or were they really masters of the art of magic, as they were accused by many of their critics? Even today it's still not clear.

The Victorians and Fake Mind Reading

Victorian clairvoyants were masters in the art of 'faking' paranormal phenomena, and some even created their own methods of stage mind-reading acts. One particular method continued to fool audiences right up to the 1940s, and although very simple, very few people managed to fathom exactly how it was done.

The 'act' involved the members of the audience writing questions for the clairvoyant, which were handed to him in individually sealed envelopes. One of the questions would be from a 'plant' in the audience; this was usually a family member or close friend, and so the clairvoyant had prior knowledge of what was written in one of the sealed envelopes.

The process of the mind-reading act was so simple. The clairvoyant had to place his hand on each sealed envelope and relate the question it contained to the audience. The writer of the question would put his or her hand up to acknowledge that it was their question, and then the clairvoyant would answer it before opening the envelope and moving on to the next one. Of course, he would begin the demonstration by relating the question his partner had written, and of which he had prior knowledge, and once his partner had confirmed that he was correct, he would then open a random envelope, thus pretending that it was the one he had just related to the audience. Of course it wasn't anything of the kind. Without anyone suspecting that he had a 'plant' in the audience, the clairvoyant was now cunningly able to read the next question, which he would then relate to the audience, pretending that he was 'psychically' probing the following randomly selected sealed envelope. And so the trickery continued. This was an extremely simple 'trick' but one that always fooled Victorian audiences. Although charlatans still exist today, generally speaking devotees of the paranormal and mediums etc are more discerning and are now wise to all the tricks of the trade. Nonetheless, some charlatans do slip through the net, so to speak, and continue to 'fool' loyal followers of the paranormal.

Chapter Nine

Psychological Phenomena

In today's psychological climate there is now very little doubt that the mind's capabilities are endless, and what psychologists actually know of the mind and the way it works can most probably be written on the back of a postage stamp. An awful lot of what is written about the mind is supposition and conjecture, as it is a mysterious part of man's metaphysical being that has baffled philosophers and mystics from time immemorial. Some esoteric schools of thought believe that the mind is located outside of the body, and is completely independent of it. This may well be true when one considers how it is possible to use the imagination to travel great distances in the vehicle of the mind. This is apparent with Meditation, which is an ideal tool with which to focus the mind and divert its attention completely away from the physical body, totally anaesthetizing it to pain and making it completely oblivious to all bodily sensations. Meditation is prescribed by many general practitioners for those suffering from stress, and even to aid recovery from cardiac arrest. While parapsychologists frequently dismiss much of the phenomena produced by mediums, clairvoyants and psychics, they will accept the psychological and emotional value of meditation and similar mental practices. There is no disputing the fact that by learning to control the mind many things can be achieved. It is fairly simple to understand the logic behind a skeptic's thinking, and if you have never experienced anything of a paranormal nature, then it is easy to dismiss. Nobody has ever actually 'seen' God, (but I'm quite sure some people will say otherwise) even though many people believe that he/she exists, even though our understanding of God today is far different from what it was when we were children. From the very moment we begin to develop an awareness of life as a child, our parental programming commences. We are indoctrinated from a very early age into a core of teachings that our parents were also indoctrinated into when they were children, and so it carries on through generation after generation. As children we are taught about religion and informed that when we die if we are good we go to heaven, and if we are bad we go to hell. In fact, the concepts of heaven and hell remain subconsciously with us all through our lives, and at death many atheists and agnostics secretly harbor the hope that they will survive death and go to heaven and not hell for their wrong beliefs. Discovering you have been wrong in your condemnation of something is one thing, but actually admitting you have been wrong is perhaps the most difficult thing to do. The psychological implications of admitting you have been wrong can be quite severe, particularly where the paranormal is concerned, which is why skeptics always vehemently dismiss mediums and clairvoyants, and parapsychologists give them the opportunity to 'prove it'. As well as the paranormal being an emotional and psychological minefield, both for its supporters and its detractors, it is also occasionally an extremely aggressive battlefield, with Christian fundamentalists on one side, skeptics and parapsychologists on another, and the devotees of the paranormal in the middle.

Mediumship Subjective

The problem with mediumistic experiences is they mostly occur subjectively, and unless the medium is able to articulate the experience in a reasonable and sensible way, then it is well and truly dismissed. Objective paranormal experiences fall within the parameters of 'believable', and providing there are sufficient people there to witness the phenomena, it can only be disputed by anyone who was not present at the time of the paranormal occurrence. It is quite funny really, but nothing will ever sway the devotees of the paranormal from believing, regardless of whether or not they have actually experienced any phenomena at all for themselves. In fact, historically some of its ardent supporters have been such notable people as Sir Arthur Conan Doyle, writer and creator of Sherlock Holmes, Sir Oliver Lodge, leading physicist, and even inventor, Benjamin Franklin. These gentlemen, and many others like them, compromised their professional positions by declaring their interest in things of a supernatural nature. So there must be something in the paranormal for it to attract such an interest, even though it is still dismissed by many skeptics as being complete and utter rubbish. In my experience, although skeptics always protest that the paranormal is ridiculous and there is nothing whatsoever in it, when engrossed in a heated conversation with them you will hear the majority of them announce, "but there was this one time... " Even skeptics have a story to tell about something that happened to them at some time in their lives. But then they always quickly add, "but whether that could be defined as paranormal, I don't really think so!"

Hypnagogic State

The majority of people have had some sort of paranormal experiences at some time in their life, albeit at a rudimentary level. I have already explained the nature of the so-called 'corner-of-the-eye' syndrome when some sort of unexplained phenomena appears in the peripheral vision, and when you turn your head to look directly at it, there is nothing whatsoever there! Most people have experienced the psychological phenomenon produced by acute fatigue, and when you are drifting into sleep images of anonymous faces quickly pass through your consciousness, or you may even find yourself listening to various disembodied voices echoing inside the chambers of your mind. The Hypnagogic state is the name describing the psychological process of actually falling asleep, and the Hypnopompic state is the psychological process of waking up, when the mind has not fully regained consciousness and is hovering somewhere between the psychological zones of being asleep and being awake. Some psychologists would explain these psychological phenomena as no more than the processing of the mind's accumulation of data, a meticulous neurological procedure during which useful information is compartmentalizing and all the rubbish is dispensed. There is no doubt about it, where the paranormal is concerned psychology is extremely useful.

Ouija Board Dangers

Have you ever wondered why some people are still sufficiently fascinated with the Ouija board, and ignore all stern warnings about its use? This surely must be down to ignorance of the very broad implications. Apart from the stern warnings that the users will summon up demonic or evil forces, there are, without a doubt, psychological factors. For example, individuals with a history of nervous or psychological disorders are extremely susceptible to obsessive paranoia and are in danger of believing that they have been 'possessed' by an evil disembodied soul. The actual belief in this is really all that is required, for as the mind is the common denominator, the imagination will do the rest. A parapsychologist's explanation for the planchette or pointer's spontaneously movement across the Ouija board is that it is the result of the psychological phenomenon ideomotor effect, involuntary movement of the muscles rather than by an external disembodied influence. So, it's a fact then, mediums and paranormal investigators just cannot win, at least where parapsychologists are concerned. And just like mediums they are truly damned if they do, and damned if they don't! Parapsychology is a pseudo-science, and a profession for which no real qualifications are actually required for the individual to practise. In saying this, there are parapsychologists and there are parapsychologists; some are clearly 'textbook' nerds, and quote verbatim from the text books they have studied, and there are those academically qualified individuals who make a serious study of the subject, carefully assessing the phenomena and the experience of others. The latter are the parapsychologists who are to be taken seriously, and not the ones who seek the exposure of television and radio and also proclaim that they are academics when they are not! What are the criteria required to be a parapsychologist?

Parapsychology and Qualification

As far as I am aware no particular qualifications are needed to begin working in the field of parapsychology, and very often there is very little difference between a paranormal investigator and a parapsychologist. As long as the paranormal investigator has the knowledge and possesses the appropriate 'ghost hunting' devices, then he or she is equally as qualified. This statement may come as a surprise to many paranormal investigators and provoke many protestations from parapsychologists. I am not suggesting that there are no qualifications available at all to be a parapsychologist; I am just saying that it is not absolutely necessary. It most certainly looks better and much more professional, but as long as you are properly equipped both with the gadgets and knowledge, then you do have the right to call yourself a parapsychologist. In fact, it is possible to do online courses in parapsychology, and many of these are conducted by parapsychologists who have either qualified in America, or have simply taken parapsychology as an extra curriculum in their psychology degree.

Whichever way you look at it, the paranormal is an incredibly vast subject and one which is still viewed by a lot of people with cynicism and disdain, and others with fear and trepidation. Unfortunately, many unscrupulous people see the paranormal as an ideal way of making easy money. And with no particular laws in place to prevent this, it is a fact that really cannot be ignored.

Chapter Ten

Psychology of the Poltergeist Phenomenon!

The growing interest in the paranormal has also caused a massive increase in the number of paranormal groups all over the world, the members of which enthusiastically devote their time searching diligently for tangible evidence that ghosts exist and that the poltergeist phenomenon is a scientific as well as a paranormal fact! Needless to say, the majority of paranormal groups are content with any commonplace sound or light anomaly, and few ever encounter any phenomenon that could truly be defined as 'paranormal', regardless of what is recorded by their EMF or any other sophisticated recording apparatus. A so-called 'poltergeist' can in actual fact take many different forms, and although the classic poltergeist phenomenon is considered very demonstrative and highly volatile, the majority of poltergeist activity produces little more than pungent smells, knocking sounds and occasional telekinetic movement of a single solid object. Probably the most famous case was the so-called 'Enfield Poltergeist' in North London. This involved two girls who lived with their mother and other siblings in a council house. The two sisters shared a bedroom and were the focus of an extremely boisterous spirit. Some of the phenomena they experienced were levitation, and furniture and smaller objects being thrown around the room. Veritable mayhem pursued, and the family life was constantly in chaos. Maurice Grosse, paranormal researcher, was consulted to investigate the phenomena, and he was so impressed with what he encountered that he devoted most of his time to making a detailed analysis of all the paranormal occurrences. The phenomena continued for some time but ceased when the girls were old enough to leave home.

No further poltergeist activity was experienced, even though the girls' mother remained in the house until she died in 1998. Since then there have been numerous books written about the Enfield Poltergeist, the majority of which have been fairly factual with bits of anecdotal information integrated into them.

Poltergeist Phenomenon – Fact or Fiction

But what exactly is a poltergeist from my perspective? Over the years I have investigated different sorts of poltergeist cases and found marked differences in the way they actually manifest. To begin with, the dictionary definition of 'poltergeist' is 'noisy, boisterous or mischievous spirit'. This definition is in actual fact only partly true! A so-called 'poltergeist' is not always the manifestation of phenomena produced by a disembodied energy source. Although the majority of cases are very often connected to mischievous or even malevolent spirits, there is a minority of poltergeist activity that is actually caused by an accumulation of bioplasmic energy – that is energy that was initially created by individuals while they were still very much alive and living at the location where the poltergeist is currently active.

Subtle Atmosphere of an Old Building

Every individual discharges minute particles of his or her own personal energies, which gradually infiltrate the subtle structure of the building where they reside. These energies build up over the years, thus creating the subtle atmosphere, a sort of invisible personality of the house itself. The subtle nature of the building then takes on the 'psychic' character of the people who live or have lived there, giving it either warmth or coldness, whichever the case may be. It is this that is 'felt' by anyone visiting there for the very first time. Generally speaking, for a house to have experienced generations of evil is comparatively rare, and so the majority of old buildings, for example, are usually just filled with character and a pleasant atmosphere, created by all those who have lived there over the years. However, there are exceptions where the subtle nature of an old building has been relentlessly bombarded by the unpleasant energies of its inhabitants through the years. Should an individual with no evil intent decide to tolerate conditions and continue to live in a house inhabited by a poltergeist, in time he or she will become totally detached psychologically, and will eventually find themselves completely absorbed by the negative energies. Of course, this condition clears once the person decides to vacate the house. In the case where a malevolent or mischievous spirit is responsible for the phenomena, one can presume that the disembodied energy has some form of rudimentary intelligence and therefore is conscious of what it is doing, where the previous case was not! The erratic and at times very aggressive behavior of the perpetrator of the phenomena is extremely difficult in this case to address, as the poltergeist is very often empowered and energized by the fear it is able to create, and so through fear its wrath is perpetuated.

Poltergeist Noises and Smells

Some of the characteristics of poltergeist phenomena are an indescribable pungent smell often accompanied by a cacophony of noises, usually knocking or thudding sounds that very often seem as though they are echoing some distance away. These alone can be quite chilling and cause the fear to gradually rise in the person experiencing it. Deep mumbling and often indistinguishable voices are also quite common. These are usually so indistinct that the victim is forced to focus his or her attention on them, at which point profanities may then be heard causing even more fear to be experienced. In the initial stages of poltergeist phenomena the telekinetic display is very often quite mild, but this too gathers momentum and then usually becomes quite fierce and very aggressive. Poltergeist phenomena is completely different from the phenomena produced by apparitions and other ghostly manifestations, inasmuch as a destructive and aggressive poltergeist usually possesses exactly the same power that it had when it occupied a physical body. The more gentle ghostly manifestation is usually only concerned with continuing his or her 'routine' and the 'habits' of their earthly life. An individual who is malevolent in this life does not suddenly change when he or she dies. Once the transition is made from this world to the next, the individual discovers that without a physical body there are few restrictions, and that it is easier to gratify his or her desires and to perpetrate with greater ease the evil deeds that fuelled them in a physical body. To some skeptics this may sound like an over-dramatization of poltergeists, but I am simply stating the very worst-case scenario. Poltergeists are very often empowered by young girls in puberty, and their energies then precipitated by female hormones that help to perpetuate their strength and power. Primarily to seize the attention of the individual, poltergeists initially appear quite playful, but once they have established their presence, the aggression usually ensues. Although many mediums do claim to have completely eradicated poltergeist activity from a building simply by talking persuasively to the offending phenomenon, in my experience all the persuasive dialogue in the world will not succeed in abolishing poltergeist activity once it has fully established itself at a location. The clearing process should be initiated over a period of time, with the poltergeist's defenses being systematically and strategically broken down through direct confrontation, which very often demobilizes its forces. Catching a poltergeist unawares with jollity and lightheartedness also helps in the whole process of disarming its negative energies and neutralizing its power. Giving a house a complete makeover, including changing the whole color arrangement of the decor certainly helps to stabilize the atmosphere. Any pungent smells need to be completely eradicated by burning pleasant incense all through the day and night. The geological phenomenon triboluminescence can also empower and encourage the strength of poltergeist activity. Where this is the case an experienced geopathic stress practitioner should be consulted to assess the level of negative energy. Above all, poltergeist activity should not be ignored or left to its own devices. Poltergeists have been known to dissipate over a period of time, but the activity can reoccur. Hollywood's hype has sensationalized the whole poltergeist phenomenon, and although the poltergeist itself cannot, generally speaking, harm the inhabitants of a household, the activity it produces can inflict serious injury if not death.

Chapter Eleven

Spiritualism – Religion of Yesterday or Science of Tomorrow?

There is no doubt about it, although Spiritualism is very often viewed with some humor and skepticism, it is one of the most interesting and fastest growing religions in the world. But what does Spiritualism really have to offer that other religions or philosophical organizations do not? To begin with, one of the fascinations of Spiritualism is the fact that each service has a medium in attendance to give 'messages' to selected members of the audience. Whether or not the interest in Spiritualism would be exactly the same if the clairvoyance part of the service was removed remains to be seen. However, one thing is for certain; Spiritualism as a religion is different to others in many ways. Where a minister or priest can only philosophize about life after death, the Spiritualist medium can, at his or her best, offer tangible evidence that we live on when we die. Over the last 50 years Spiritualism has done well to struggle from beneath the heavy weight of religious dogma and public criticism, and today stands proud as one of the most interesting religions in the world.

Problematic Spiritualism

But, is Spiritualism completely free from the problems found in many other mainstream religions, such as jealousy, conflict and the cliquey element? Some years ago now I served as the president of Southport Spiritualist Church, one of the most prestigious Spiritualist Churches in the North West of England. I held that position for two years and this had to be the most difficult and thankless task I have ever had to face, and a position

I would not wish on my worst enemy. Although initially I was asked to take up the presidency to initiate important changes, in a very short time, primarily because I would not kowtow to the committee members, they began to make life very difficult for me. Needless to say, I did initiate many changes in the church and did everything in my power to increase the membership and make the church more attractive to a younger congregation. I did this and more. Under great opposition I also introduced a Christmas morning service, which cynics said would not work. To everyone's surprise more than 50 people attended the service, which was a great success. Under extreme pressure from the committee, and a so-called 'extraordinary' meeting, I resigned from my position as president. Needless to say, that was the very first and last Christmas morning service at Southport Spiritualist Church. Apart from my brief sojourn as church president, I still continued to serve Spiritualist Churches all over the UK. Although I found many Spiritualist Churches were friendly and extremely warm, the majority of them were cliquey and unfriendly. If your face does not fit, then some Spiritualist Churches most definitely make it extremely difficult for a person to become actively involved in the running of things. There is no doubt that the running of a Spiritualist Church requires a particular skill, and this includes knowing how to deal with people on all levels, particularly those seeking support through bereavement and other emotionally difficult periods. The majority of those who run Spiritualist Churches are most certainly not qualified for any of these things and should not therefore be allowed to run the church. Through the last 50 years or more, many notable people have believed in and supported Spiritualism, and some of these have compromised their professional integrity in doing so. It is not difficult to see the attraction of Spiritualism, as it offers the opportunity to explore the concept of life beyond death, and to study such spiritual skills as mediumship, Spiritual healing and the science of psychic development. In theory, Spiritualism has an awful lot to offer without expecting an individual to abandon his or her own religion. In my opinion, Spiritualism is more a philosophical way of life than it is a religion, and is really the foundation upon which all religions are based. One thing that many Spiritualists find offensive is the claim that Spiritualism is an 'Occult' religion. It is just that by virtue of the fact that it does permit such metaphysical practices as clairvoyance and spiritual healing. The actual word 'occult' is nearly always taken completely out of context, and today its meaning is perhaps not as severe as it was 50 years ago. Among other things, the dictionary defines the word as 'supernatural phenomena', as well as 'hidden' or 'secret'. However, most people relate the word 'occult' to 'black magic' or 'witchcraft', a connotation that is perhaps today slightly misleading. Regardless of what people may think, walking through the doors of a Spiritualist Church is not quite the same as walking through the doors of any of the orthodox churches, at least for anyone who has not attended one of its services before. Spiritualism does have an air of mystery for first timers, and the Spiritualist service always creates overwhelming feelings of expectancy, something one does not experience in an orthodox church.

Mediums Serve Spiritualist Churches

The majority of mediums today have served their 'apprenticeship' on the Spiritualist Church circuit; but as there are no special qualifications required for a person to begin working as a professional medium, serving an apprenticeship on the Spiritualist circuit is not a prerequisite. In saying this, many people see the Spiritualist Church route much easier when seeking a platform for their mediumistic skills. The majority of churches welcome 'new blood', particularly young developing mediums, who they find much easier to cultivate and indoctrinate into the Spiritualist philosophy. However, there has always been a minority of Spiritualist Churches who tend to cling to the 'old' ways and very often resent new faces. These are the diehard Spiritualists who prevent the Spiritualist movement as a whole from moving into more modern times. Many of the more modern thinking Spiritualists have removed the word 'church' to be replaced with the less religious description of 'center', more inviting to the younger element.

In my opinion Spiritualism is the science of the future, and although today it is the foundation upon which all religions are based, tomorrow it will be the key to a more fulfilled Spiritual way of life, and will succeed where all other religions will have failed.

In fact, in *The Lyceum Manual*, the Spiritualist book for children, it says of Spiritualism: *"It is the aim of Spiritualism to affect a complete at-one-ment and unison of man with God, until every thought and action of man is in perfect harmony with the divine will."* To my mind, of Spiritualism there is nothing else to be said.

Chapter Twelve

The Polygraph and the Deluded Medium

As I have previously stated in an earlier chapter, there has always been a big problem with 'fake' mediums, depending that is on what you define as 'fake'. Even the skills of some so-called 'high profile' mediums are somewhat suspicious and would not stand-up to close scrutiny. As a medium I am able to look closely at another medium's technique, style and methodology, and am able to identify which parts of a 'message' do not originate from a discarnate source.

Cold Reading

A so-called 'psychic' message that is not genuine is slightly more difficult to detect, as even what parapsychologists describe as 'cold reading' can appear extremely specific, particularly when the recipient of it gives an enthusiastic and very positive response. Whether or not they admit it, all mediums use what are termed 'fillers' – pieces of general dialogue that are used either to make a message more interesting, or simply to fill-in where there are pauses in the delivery of the message. These so-called fillers can be anything from clichéd pieces of dialogue, to general remarks about the individual's lifestyle etc. I have previously stated that mediumistic skills are inconsistent and very unreliable, and so it is therefore often necessary to expand the information by 'adding' other insignificant dialogue to it, or even 'ad-libbing' to make the message much more attractive to listen to.

Message 'Fillers'

This oral device is a skill that all mediums must learn if they are ever to be proficient at his or her craft. When I conduct courses or workshops for those endeavoring to be mediums, in the initial stages I focus primarily on stagecraft, technique and style, rather than concentrate first of all on the actual mediumistic ability. In my experience I have found that once the public persona has been cultivated, including style and presentation, then the inherent skills usually flourish as a direct result. This approach is not always understood by those who desperately want to work as mediums, but once they have accepted my method of teaching they quickly understand and are able to see the motive behind it all. Once again, it is quite easy to see the psychology behind the actual mechanics of mediumship, and as long as the fundamental principles underlying the process of mediumship are fully understood, then both the skeptic and the developing medium will be able to appreciate and comprehend what the actual process of giving a mediumistic message is really all about. Skeptics are more concerned about discrediting mediums and psychics than they are about exploring the possibilities of whether or not any of it really genuinely works. It is very true that knowledge is power, and so if mediums prepared themselves with knowledge of their mediumistic skills, the argument would be won, primarily because the skeptic would have nothing whatsoever to argue about.

Fake Mediums

What exactly constitutes a 'fake' medium? Well, although the majority are fairly obvious, a small minority become so proficient at putting it over that sometimes it is quite difficult to determine whether he or she is a fake. I mentioned in an earlier chapter that many people confuse a pleasant personality with good mediumship. Sometimes a personable manner and professional presentation cleverly conceal the fact that the individual is not genuine. Although not all people are gullible, unless the person is not afraid to speak his or her mind, the majority ignore their instincts and agree with the consensus. Because the quality of mediumship is today generally quite poor, mediums eager to pursue a mediumistic profession have no one really with whom to draw a real comparison, and so they mistakenly believe that what they are demonstrating is in fact genuine mediumship.

Lie Detector

However, this suggests that those whose mediumship is of an inferior quality are deluding themselves and deceiving all those who come to see them demonstrating their abilities. One suggestion was to subject all mediums to the polygraph (lie detector), one would think a sure way of sorting out the wheat from chaff. However, it has already been proven that the majority of so-called 'fake' mediums are so deluded, and believe in their own skills to such an extent, that even such a scientific device as the polygraph would not be sufficient to 'catch' the medium out! To be quite honest, a genuine medium can only be judged on the accuracy and content of the messages he or she is able to give. The delivery of the fake medium's demonstration will most certainly be hit-and-miss, and the content of the messages they give would most probably be subject to chance and probability, where the genuine medium's messages will not. I suppose it makes a lot of sense that you can only make a judgment when you receive a message yourself. And even then the whole thing depends on the content and quality of the information you are given. Even when the medium's messages appear extremely accurate, it is sometimes extremely difficult to make a rational judgment as to whether or not he or she is genuine and truly receiving the information from a disembodied source. As I have already said in a previous chapter, a medium can be so popular and well-liked that they have the total support of the audience, and so therefore cannot in anyway put a foot wrong! Of course, it can work the other way for a medium. It matters very little how accurate their information actually is, should the audience not like their manner, for whatever reason, then their demonstration of mediumship is just not going to work. I have seen this so many times, and have even experienced it for myself. In this case the recipients of my messages approached me at the conclusion of the show to tell me how accurate my message to them actually was. Of course, like all mediums, I am more concerned with the responses I receive during my demonstrations, and although it is a relief to learn that my messages were not wrong, if the recipient did not have the good grace and manners to give a positive response so everyone could hear it during the show, then I usually show my displeasure with a curt "Thank you!" As I have already said, audiences at a theater psychic show can be extremely aggressive, hostile and very rude especially if they don't receive a message or if they don't like the look of the medium. This might sound a little far-fetched, but believe me it is true. On the other hand, the majority of those who attend theater shows are very polite and treat a medium's performance with respect and very often in an almost reverential way. Today mediums are revered almost like pop or film stars, and the majority of high profile mediums do attract a huge fan following. The majority of mediums do work to a code of ethics and will always admit when they are wrong. However, there is a minority of unscrupulous individuals who masquerade as mediums and whose sole intention is to make as much money as possible, as well as to become well-known as mediums. Should you be interested in mediums and psychics, the onus is on you to be keenly vigilant and to question at all times anything that does not seem right, regardless of how popular the medium is.

Chapter Thirteen

When Is a Medium Not a Medium?

The term 'New Age' has today become synonymous with many esoteric subjects, ranging from Chakras to the Aura, from Angels to Channeling. In fact, New Age subjects are extremely fashionable and the devotees of such a trend are increasing in numbers each year. Of course, New Age is an umbrella term for all things esoteric and anything else that has seemingly filtered in from the USA. In fact, America is always the first to begin a trend, and the UK always the first to expand upon it, giving it credibility and longevity. One such Americanism is so-called 'channeling', another descriptive term for 'trance'. Although channeling practitioners and New Age devotees would argue that channeling and trance are two very different concepts, in principle they are one and the same. At least, the process of each is the same, even though to my mind channeling is far easier to fake. Trance mediumship does not develop overnight and really does take time and require a great deal of patience.

Channeling

Working in trance is not a skill that anyone can develop, and just because a person is mediumistically inclined does not mean that he or she can develop the ability to work in trance. Before we move any further, let us explore the concepts of channeling and trance, and then make a detailed analysis of their differences. From a Spiritualistic perspective, trance is the ability possessed by some mediums to allow a disembodied personality to take control of his or her consciousness and to speak through them. Witnessing genuine trance mediumship is an experience, as one is able to see a remarkable transformation as the medium slowly slips into a somnambulistic state of consciousness to allow the disembodied personality to take control. The difference between the before and after states is quite astonishing. In a demonstration of genuine trance mediumship, one is able to question the controlling personality about the period he or she lived in. This is where the one who is faking it usually fails to impress. One would expect a disembodied personality from shall we say the seventeenth century to answer any questions about that period. Unless, of course, the individual has done their research and is prepared for all eventualities, then they are not so easy to expose.

Madame Tickel and Trance

I once witnessed a frail and very elderly lady give a demonstration of remarkable trance mediumship, during which she became a middle-aged Victorian doctor. All those present watched mesmerized as the lady's delicate and stooping form metamorphosed into a strong and very upright, stern looking individual, with a voice that issued forth, filling the spacious church hall. Madame Tickel gave an exceptional demonstration of trance mediumship, and she was even able to answer medical questions put to her by each member of the small group. She allowed three very different discarnate entities to control her, each from a different historical period, and each time impressing the small group by answering questions from the period each discarnate personality represented. Unfortunately, Madame Tickel passed away several months later, a deep loss to the world of Spiritualism.

Queenie Nixon and Transfiguration

During my investigation of Spiritualism and mediums, I saw many so-called trance mediums who failed miserably to impress me. Some fell into trance at the drop of a hat, and others made no effort at all to conceal the fact that they were faking it. Then I was fortunate to have a private consultation with world-renowned transfiguration medium Queenie Nixon from Derby, England. In trance she was an articulate, well-spoken Victorian lady, who not only brought my father to me, but passed on information to me that nobody but me knew. My father never, ever called me by name; he either called me 'lad' or 'babs', terms of endearment that he had used from my early childhood right up until the day he died in 1970. As I was the last of her clients for the day, she allowed me to sit with her while she came out of trance, a state of consciousness she had maintained for at least four hours. To my great surprise, when she 'returned' and opened her eyes, she spoke with a broad Derbyshire accent and even looked completely different. Even her eyes seemed to shine with a completely different spirit, and were no longer cold and stern, as they had been throughout the consultation. Unlike many trance mediums, Queenie Nixon's eyes had remained open while she was in trance, a feature that seems to be adopted by some genuine trance mediums. On that particular visit to a Spiritualist Church in Liverpool, England, I was also fortunate to witness Queenie Nixon give an incredible public demonstration of Transfiguration. This is where the medium (in trance) goes to selected members of the congregation with a message, during which the medium's face transfigures with the face of the 'dead' person from whom the message is given. Although I have no doubt that Queenie Nixon was a genuine trance medium, I have seen many so-called transfiguration demonstrations that have been extremely suspicious to say the least.

Trance mediumship takes many years of dedication, patience and determination to fully develop. One knows instinctively when a trance medium is genuine, and everything about them changes dramatically. In more recent years one so-called 'high profile' television medium has been seen falling into a trance at the drop of a hat, sometimes appearing very aggressive and shouting profanities at the presenter of the television program.

The exhibition of such histrionics brings the whole thing into disrepute and also misinforms viewers about the realities of trance mediumship. In the case of the aforementioned medium, somewhere along the line they changed the description of his demonstration from 'trance' to 'obsession'. Either way, these states just do not happen as spontaneously.

Channeling seems to be the new trance and, unlike the trance state, exponents of so-called 'channeling' have been known to go through the process of channeling quite spontaneously and without great effort. Although it's only my opinion, in a lot of cases channeling is highly suspicious, and unless the medium can channel information that he or she would not normally be capable of giving, then the whole thing is pretty pointless. Over the past few years or so I have also witnessed channeling being brought into disrepute. One medium in particular claimed he was able to channel the spirit of Beatle John Lennon, and while he was appearing on an American television program the presenter asked, "What does John have to say then?" The medium (who shall remain nameless for obvious reasons) simply announced, "Give peace a chance!" Yeah, right! What more can I say?

In the marketing of his shows, one medium states that he was trained by an Eastern 'Mystery School', whatever that has do with mediumship! I think the medium in question should have done more research. Had he done so he would have known that the majority of so-called 'Mystery Schools' were in fact dissolved over 1500 years ago.

Another fairly well-known medium claimed to channel the spirits of Elvis Presley and Liverpool's 1950s/60s singer, Billy Fury. As well as being a medium, the man in question had also been a professional singer, and so this was the perfect opportunity for him to sing, one would think, just like the dead singers. I heard a recording of both personalities he allegedly 'channeled' and their voices sounded no different to the voice of the medium himself. The voices were not even good impersonations of either of the two crooners. Apart from everything else this sort of mimicry causes the whole profession of channeling and trance mediumship to be ridiculed and brings it into disrepute. Thankfully not everyone is gullible and the majority of people are able to see it for what it is, 'fake' mediumship at its worst! I do realize that I will be criticized by the diehard supporters of such mediums for writing this, but some things do have to be said, don't you agree?

The Mediumship of Bill Angus

In the 1950s the trance demonstrations of a medium from Wirral, England were always well attended. Billy Angus (a friend of mine) would become entranced by the spirit of a Scottish clergyman who gave his name as John Barclay. As Bill Angus was an extremely inquisitive man, he needed desperately to know if John Barclay ever existed, or if he was simply a figment of his own imagination. Before going into trance one particular night, Bill instructed those present to ask the spirit control, John Barclay, specific questions, to enable him to investigate the man's identity further. John Barclay was quite specific with his answers and told everyone present the name of the church he preached at in a remote part of Scotland, in the mid eighteenth century, and said that he was also buried there. He also said that a book had been written about him, one chapter of which was completely inaccurate. John Barclay requested that once the grave had been located, Bill Angus should do everything he could to change the text in the appropriate chapter of the book, and replace it with the correct information.

Strangely enough, Bill Angus had always felt an affinity with Scotland and knew John Barclay's area very well. Although it took some time, he eventually located the church and John Barclay's overgrown grave. And although getting the chapter changed in the now out-of-print book was more difficult, with so much evidence to support his claims Bill eventually persuaded the publishers to reprint the book about John Barclay, along with the newly revised chapter. Although I never had the good fortune to witness Bill Angus in trance, his reputation as a trance medium was known all over the UK. He was so popular that he was asked to give a well-known personality a trance reading at a location in Southport. Bill Angus was taken to a large Georgian house in the suburbs of Southport, where he waited patiently in the library for his guest to arrive. Half an hour later a helicopter landed on the back lawn, and Bill was amazed to see the comedic film star Peter Sellers climbing from it. It is no secret that Peter Sellers had a deep interest in mediums and the paranormal. As Bill Angus was in trance for the duration of Peter's Seller's sitting, he was unable to recall exactly what transpired. However, whatever happened in Southport that day in the late 1950s, Peter Sellers was said to be exceedingly pleased with his consultation and left the house shaking his head in disbelief.

With so many pressures imposed on him by spending so much time working in trance, Bill announced that he had decided to call it a day and part company with his long time friend, John Barclay. He gave his last demonstration of trance mediumship at the Psychic Truth Society in Liverpool, to a capacity audience consisting of journalists and researchers. While in trance the onlookers were amazed as the blindfolded Bill Angus (to eliminate the possibility of trickery) scribbled copperplate text on a blackboard, his hand moving so fast that witnesses were scarcely able to follow the chalk as the words appeared in reversed order, one after the other. Why such demonstrations of trance mediumship are not seen today is not really clear, and what purports to be genuine trance is very often no more than a demonstration of poor acting or blatant pretense.

Chapter Fourteen

Living With Angels and Demons

As someone who has had a deep interest in the paranormal since I was very young, I do know only too well that it can be a psychological minefield where some people are concerned. Some individuals see the paranormal as little more than a hobby, while others look upon it as something that must be feared and treated with a great deal of respect. Whichever way you perceive it, the paranormal is most definitely a fact of life, and encompasses the psychological as well as the spiritual aspects of human experience. I have always found it extremely interesting how differently we humans perceive a paranormal experience. An apparition may be looked upon by one person as an angelic visitation, while another will see it as a manifestation of evil and something that must be exorcised. There is no doubt about it, the way we perceive things as adults is solely dependent upon the way we have been influenced by our parents and social circumstances when we were children.

Perception Influenced by Religion

A well-balanced, religious upbringing more than likely makes us stay clear of all things paranormal when we are adults, and also to fear those things we do not quite understand. However, a religious individual will either perceive a ghostly apparition as an angelic presence and something that must be revered and treated with a great deal of respect, or perhaps see it as something that is quite evil and threatening. "Let the dead rest!" is the usual indictment made by those who do not fully understand what an apparition is exactly. "It is wrong to mess around with things we do not understand!" is another statement that is frequently made. And how very true that is! We should not play with things we don't understand, particularly where some paranormal phenomena are concerned. But there has to be something far more than upbringing that influences the way we perceive things of a paranormal nature, don't you think? Some people have an inherent dread of the unknown, while others seem intrigued and fascinated by it. The mind is undoubtedly the common denominator where the paranormal is concerned, and how it is perceived is purely subjective and so varies from individual to individual. The mind is so powerful a tool, that sometimes to imagine what you see is to actually create it, even though it wasn't really there in the first place. And so, can involvement in the paranormal really affect some individuals adversely? If so, how and why? Well, to begin with it is true that those of a nervous disposition are easily affected by even the most rudimentary form of paranormal phenomena, and even those who treat such things lightheartedly, ignoring any dangers, may well be psychologically affected at a more subtle level, without them even realizing it. The paranormal cannot be ignored and should at all times be taken seriously. One thing is for certain, the dead do not really die! Where they actually reside after death is another question, about which we can only hypothesize, even though the majority of mediums offer a valid and very detailed description of what the afterlife is really like. Do the dead actually go anywhere? It has already been established that the human organism is an electromagnetic unit of incredible power, assimilating, transmuting and discharging energy, and is also contained within its own spectrum of color and light.

Science and Internal Space

Over the last ten years science has begun to explore internal as well as external space, and many researchers have reached the conclusion that man is far more than a collection of cells, the total manifestation of which experiences a life-expectancy of three score years and ten, to then be subjected to complete annihilation with what we have come to know as 'death'. Even the non-scientific person knows that energy can only be transmuted into a different form and not destroyed completely. Working on the premise that the human organism is a veritable powerhouse of energy, we must then assume that this too cannot be completely eradicated! In fact, there is actually no such state as death! There is only change, transmutation, growth, becoming a movement of matter or of consciousness from one condition to another.

Good and Evil After Death

Nothing can ever die! This being the case then the energies of both good and evil persist after death, each gravitating to their own individual vibratory space in the universe. Someone who is evil in this life is very often more so when he or she passes over and likewise can be said of a person who has lived an exemplary, untarnished life. Although the concepts of heaven and hell are terms that were more than likely created in pagan times primarily to explain the great vibratory divide between good and evil, it is not too difficult to understand the phenomenon of vibration in relation to the different vibratory spheres. As children it was clearly put to us that at death good people went up to heaven and those with a propensity towards evil went directly to hell. This is also witnessed in the biblical narration of Jesus when he said, "In my father's house are there many mansions!" Here he was clearly suggesting that there are many varying degrees of vibration in the supersensual universe, and the more spiritually developed individuals at death ascend to the higher, more refined vibratory planes of existence, and the less spiritually inclined, being of a lower frequency of vibration, descend into the denser slower vibratory regions of the darker planes of existence. Although these explanations seem to complicate things a little for some people, it is really a very simple analogy that defines very precisely the whole process of good and evil after death. But then, how does all this affect us while we are still living on a dense, three-dimensional planet in an environment of earth, sky and human habitations? The human mind is to all intents and purposes the portal to the vastness of the vibratory frontiers of the supersensual universe, and once focused, even taking into account the law of attraction, it does not in any way discriminate between the forces it attracts. And so, the very fact that you have become involved in the paranormal simply means that your mind is open to both negative and positive influences. Unfortunately, the majority of paranormal devotees are completely oblivious to the many implications of being involved with the paranormal, and little do they also realize that to acknowledge is to empower the very forces they are mentally touching upon. Evil forces will always seek minds of a similar vibration for the gratification of their desires. You may protest, "Well I am not in any way evil so I am all right!" Believe me this is not sufficient to afford you protection. As your mind does not discriminate between good and evil, neither do these forces discriminate, and both good and evil energies will always seek a means of gratification. The same laws that work for you also work for good and evil energies, whose battle is relentless with the forces of evil occasionally being victorious. You may dismiss this theory without any great consideration, but it is one that has been expounded by some of the greatest philosophers and occult practitioners from time immemorial.

Calling Up the Forces of Evil

I have seen some paranormal investigators calling up the forces of evil simply to sensationalize the television program in which they were taking part. The ramifications of such an invocation can nearly always prove to be catastrophic, the effects of which may not be immediate, but may occur months or even years later. Calling upon evil forces when they are not actually there simply creates and empowers them, and where the laws of the universe are concerned, this is all that is required for the demons to be sent forth. I have actually witnessed this firsthand, and although the people in question cannot be named, the ritual of calling up evil really did have its repercussions some time later.

Although a little knowledge is very dangerous, it can on rare occasions have its advantages. 'Ignorance is very often bliss' as the old saying goes, particularly as it secures the portal to the invisible worlds where both angels and demons lurk.

Angel Visitation

A young woman in Liverpool saw a bright golden light in her living room, and as she watched mesmerized, it slowly metamorphosed into what appeared to her like an angel. The young woman in question photographed it with her mobile phone and sent it to me to take a look at. Although I wasn't present when she took the photograph I had to admit that it did look like an angelic form. However, no more than a week later a fire broke out in the room where the visitation had occurred. Luckily the fire was quickly extinguished and nobody was hurt. Now, we can look at the apparition from two very different perspectives, one from the young woman's and the other from a priest who reviewed the case. The young woman saw the apparition as an angelic visitation coming to forewarn her about the fire, while the priest's explanation was that the apparition was demonic, masquerading as an angel and the very cause of the fire. On the other hand, from my mediumistic perspective I saw the apparition as a celestial or angelic being who had coincidentally warned her of the approaching potential disaster. However, I am quite certain that some priests would have seen the visitation as angelic and good, and the experience may well have been seen by any other young woman as quite evil and demonic. It is all down to our own particular belief and how the experience affects us at the actual time of the occurrence.

Thought Dynamics

The various waves of thoughts we discharge during the course of the day attract and are attracted by thoughts of a similar nature. They form *thought strata* in the psychic space, in very much the same way that clouds fall into groups in the atmosphere. This does not mean that each stratum of thought can only occupy one particular portion of space with the exclusion of all other thought clouds. On the contrary, the thought clouds are of different degrees of vibration, and so the same space may be filled with thought matter of a thousand kinds, passing freely without interference. Districts, towns and cities are permeated by the thoughts of the people who live or have lived there throughout the years, perpetuating whatever emotions created them in the first place, and consistently bombarding the minds of all those who live within the confines of their radiance. Nations constantly stricken by famine and war are forever locked within the confines of the negative radiations of the thoughts and emotions created by past inhabitants, making it impossible for them ever to recover from their relentless plight. Whether you are aware of it or not, you are being silently influenced by the unseen forces of the environment in which you live. Of course, not all invisible forces are evil; but the dominant forces of evil are much more noticeable and really do appear to be more powerful! Of one thing you can be certain, evil is more insidious and has the power to infiltrate your life in many ways. The warning is quite stern: do not treat the paranormal lightheartedly, and when you venture from the light into the darkness, tread with great caution for you will never know who or what you will meet along the way.

Chapter Fifteen

The Famous and the Paranormal

Along with many other notable Victorians, Charles Dickens was fascinated with mediums and the very fashionable séance phenomenon that was sweeping Great Britain at the time. As an integral part of the research for one of his books, he came to Liverpool where he took a temporary position as a 'special' constable patrolling the Liverpool streets. Although he was in Liverpool for a comparatively short time, he allegedly visited more than one medium, again as an integral part of the research for one of his books. Also, like many famous writers and composers, Dickens claimed that he frequently felt as though the inspiration for some of his works came from a higher, celestial source. As with many other successful people, Dickens was known to have believed in angels, and also believed that many of his deceased friends were still alive and maintained their friendship with him from another world. Dickens once said that Liverpool was his second favorite city next to London, which is why he frequently visited it to give readings from his latest works.

Oliver Lodge

Even before the death of his son, Raymond, physicist Oliver Lodge had a deep interest in mediums, and even compromised his professional integrity by making his interest publically known. Of course, after his son was killed in the First World War Oliver Lodge made a point of visiting many mediums in an attempt to maintain the strong relationship he had always enjoyed with the son he dearly loved. It is also known that the notable scientist devoted part of his life's work trying to scientifically prove life after death, and even wrote more than one book on the subject. The Spiritualist Association of Great Britain (SAGB) has a room named after him in their center in Belgrave Square, London.

Arthur Conan Doyle

It is now common knowledge that Arthur Conan Doyle, the creator of Sherlock Holmes, also had an interest in mediums and the paranormal and in fact befriended many famous mediums of his day. Of course, Conan Doyle's interest was not confined to mediums alone; he in fact had an interest in a broad spectrum of unusual phenomena, from fairies to many other areas of the paranormal.

Maurice Maeterlinck

Nineteenth century Belgium dramatist and mystic, Maurice Maeterlinck, writer of the famous play *The Bluebird* was fascinated by Spiritism, the French equivalent of Spiritualism. In fact, Maeterlinck wrote many mystical works in which he made reference to mediums and the afterlife. One of his most famous books, a mystical essay titled *Treasure of the Humble*, called upon his many paranormal experiences. Maeterlinck also believed that he was guided by angelic forces, the source of his many inspirational writings.

Peter Sellers

As stated in a previous chapter, comedic actor Peter Sellers was also extremely interested in mediums, and had a fascination with the afterlife. Sellers had an inherent fear of death and it is believed that it was this that led him to explore the world of mediums and the paranormal.

Michael Bentine

Michael Bentine, fellow Goon, comedic actor and the author of many books, also had a serious interest in the paranormal. Bentine, however, claimed to have mediumistic skills, which he frequently referred to in television and radio interviews. Bentine also wrote a couple of bestselling books on the paranormal, highlighting his psychic experiences.

Poets

Poets Keats, Shelley and Wordsworth all believed that their inspiration originated from a celestial and disembodied source, and frequently referred to this divine inspiration when discussing their work to friends.

Robert Louis Stephenson

Robert Louis Stephenson, creator of *Treasure Island*, among many other classics, attributed his inspirations to disembodied souls as well as guardian angels. Stephenson fell into poor health early in life, and even then believed that he had been visited by his 'dead' ancestors.

Edgar Allen Poe

It is now common knowledge that the author of many macabre poems and stories, Edgar Allen Poe, was also in touch with the 'other side'. In fact, his fascination with the supernatural affected him to such a degree that even his closest friends thought he was quite strange. Poe was orphaned when his mother died when he was very young. He believed that his 'dead' mother frequently visited him throughout his life, but cynics accused him of hallucinations induced by his over-indulgence of narcotics and alcohol. Poe was also deeply affected by the death of his cousin, Virginia Clemm, whom he married when she was only 13 years old. To this day Edgar Allen Poe's death at the age of 40 still remains a mystery. However, his stories and poems live on to this day, immortalizing the great writer's name in the genre of the macabre.

Queen Victoria and Mediums

Even Queen Victoria's interest in mediums was common knowledge at the time. After the death of her husband Prince Albert in 1861, it is said that Queen Victoria maintained her relationship with him through various mediums whom she summoned to visit her at the palace. One such medium was Robert Lees, whom it is said would go into trance allowing the Queen to hold long conversations with her 'dead' husband. Although it cannot be fully corroborated, it is believed that Robert Lees helped Victorian police unsuccessfully with their search for Jack the Ripper. It was also suggested that it was Lees who introduced John Brown to Queen Victoria, after he himself had declined to make any more visits to the palace. Although it is mostly anecdotal, many friends of Robert Lees suggested that John Brown became Queen Victoria's personal medium as well as her closest friend and companion, a relationship that even today has given rise to many speculations.

Even today many celebrities consult clairvoyants and mediums on a fairly regular basis, and some will not even make any major decisions without first of all consulting their own personal 'seer'. Many people who dismiss mediums and clairvoyants as 'rubbish' can't resist taking a sly look at the daily astrological forecast in the morning newspaper, just to see how their day is going to go. There is very little doubt that there is something in the human psyche that makes us want to know what the future holds. Even those who announce, "I'd rather not know what's in my future, thank you very much," nearly always show an interest when something positive is said about them regarding their future. Although there is something in the human psychological makeup that makes us fear the unknown, when the actual result is positive, then remarkably attitudes change!

Chapter Sixteen

Not All Angels Have Wings!

Although man has had a belief in angels from time immemorial, it is really only over the past ten years or so that there has been a fashionable boom in the angel phenomenon, to the extent that many writers on the subject claim to be 'angel experts'. How can anyone be an angel 'expert', you may well ask? Even my book, *The Angels' Book of Promises*, is only a detailed analysis of angels and the celestial kingdoms, and although I have believed in angels since I was a child, I can hardly say that I am an expert. Nonetheless, judging by the hundreds of books about angels available in bookshops today, the interest in the subject is quite remarkable. Even those who quickly dismiss mediums and all things paranormal openly admit to believing in angels and other celestial beings. Even if you cynically dismiss angels as being no more than farfetched and fanciful, born out of the wishful thinking of the weak and the poor, they have nonetheless always been there relentlessly in every culture and throughout every age. It is true that those who believe in angels do have their own ideas of what they look like, and those who simply accept them as integral parts of their own religion see them as the archetypal beings with which we have been brought up, winged with angelic faces. If you do cynically dismiss the very idea of angels, then where did the concept of celestial visitors originate?

Angels and Medieval Artists

Angels were depicted by medieval artists as winged beings, enabling them to traverse quickly between heaven and earth, in their relentless and tireless plight to help man in times of great need. But although angels have, through the passage of time, become a fact of life, in very much the same way as God, they are collectively an integral part of human psychology, inasmuch as nobody has ever seen either God or angels, but it doesn't stop us believing in them! I know that many people have had, at some time in their lives, a transcendental experience that they have interpreted as being with angels or God; but there is only a very select minority that can actually claim to have seen either one or the other. And even then the experience has been in very unusual circumstances, such as illness or extreme psychological trauma. Still, there is an overwhelming human need for God and angels to exist. The majority of people would most probably have no difficulty in managing without the existence of angels, but would most definitely be psychologically distraught if it were proven beyond doubt that God does not exist! God is genetically encoded into the very fabric of our being; it is what very often motivates and allows us to focus in prayer. The very existence of God in our lives is what gives us a conscience and encourages us to live to a moral code and ethics. We are programmed from an early age to believe that God is all-seeing. He is omnipotent, omnipresent and omniscient, and plays an integral part in every-thing we do. We praise God for the good things that happen in our lives, and we blame Him for disasters and world catastrophes, and everything else that goes wrong in our lives. To enable us to praise and worship Him, we erect magnificent temples and churches allowing us to feel as though we are actually in his presence. Although it is against biblical teachings, we create images to represent him, such as saints and other similar symbols. Because we do not really have any idea what God actually looks like, each religion has created its own deities to symbolically represent Him primarily for our own under-standing. But then, occasionally we witness incredible kindness and benevolence to the impoverished of the world, and then we are privileged to glimpse an angel in human form, or a manifes-tation of God's love in one human being, albeit extremely rare.

Not all angels have wings, this much is abundantly clear when we are in the presence of some individuals who have nothing really in their own lives, but what they do have they are willing to give to others in need. What is it about human psychology that makes some individuals want to give everything they have to those less fortunate, and yet others with plenty are miserly and live selfish and very often cruel existences? It was once said, "If God did not exist we would need to invent him." There is a lot more truth in this statement than you realize, and God is much more of a reality than many of us would care to admit.

Divine Help

On rare occasions, perhaps when we are going through extreme trauma in our lives, a helping hand appears seemingly from nowhere. This very often unexplainable lifeline appears just when we cannot take any more. Because of the psychological and emotional trauma we are going through we quite easily attribute the help, in whatever form it comes, to the intervention of God or His angelic ambassadors, when in actual fact, it might simply have been a case of coincidence. The way we perceive these experiences differs from person to person, and it is perhaps only one in a thousand people who would dismiss such unexpected help as some sort of Divine intervention. There is something within the human psyche that is connected to a relationship with God, and in times of great need even the agnostic and the atheist silently cries out to God for help! I've no doubt that the atheist would deny this and the agnostic would say it is possible. Nonetheless, when you consider the way human nature actually works, the Eastern concept, 'there is a spark of the divine within us all', appears most certainly to be true!

Some Believe in Mediums and Some Don't

But, what is the problem many people have with mediums and their claim to be able to receive communication from the so-called 'dead'? What is it that makes some people believe in mediums and makes others completely dismiss them? If mediums cannot communicate with the souls of the disembodied, then where did the concept of mediums originate in the first place? The majority of people do accept the existence of angels, primarily because we have been indoctrinated into the celestial phenomenon from our earliest days at school. Because we were introduced to the concept of angels at a very early age it is more difficult for us to dismiss. Like God, angels are encoded into our genetic memory and are almost an integral part of what makes us human. Atheists can rarely offer a valid reason why they are absolutely certain there is no such power as God, and that death is the end! What is the psychology that motivates parapsychologists to investigate phenomena that they do not believe exists in the first place. I know that this is not the case with all parapsychologists, as some do have a serious interest in the paranormal. However, the majority of parapsychologists are ready to dismiss all phenomena with a rational explanation without even considering a supernatural cause.

First World War Angel Visitation

Many of our beliefs about angels have originated from the Shamanic traditions, particularly the idea that a *white feather* is actually the calling card of an angel. The fact that angels have appeared to those in great need was especially apparent in the First World War when a White Angel led soldiers through the gas-filled trenches to safety. In fact, there have been many stories of how angelic beings have led young soldiers away from the battlefield to safety. However, when in the grip of terror, there is always the possibility that we see something that is not really there; and there is an element in human psychology that makes us embroider a story to make it more appealing. I am certain that this is the case with the majority of paranormal experiences, and a psychological phenomenon that is employed by the majority of alleged mediums when delivering a message. In the long term the imagination plays an extremely important part in all paranormal experiences, and without an active imagination the process of clairvoyance would simply not work effectively, and 'seeing' any sort of apparition would never occur!

Chapter Seventeen

The Transcendental Experience

From time immemorial religious cultures throughout the world have used hallucinogenic substances to encourage altered states of consciousness, thus allowing a greater relationship with God and their dead ancestors. Many of the ancient seers relied upon strange herbal concoctions to induce trance-like states through which they would obtain glimpses of the future.

Shamanic Priests and Hallucinogens

Shamanic priests frequently imbibed the sacred mushroom, amanita muscaria, which would quickly encourage transcendental experiences and allow them to access other sacred dimensions. To induce their transcendental states, the Aztec priests imbibed the nectar extracted from peyote, the globe-shaped spineless cactus. Hallucinogens are known to affect the pineal gland (walnut shaped), one of the endocrine glands situated beneath the back part of the corpus callosum, and which secretes the hormone melatonin into the bloodstream. As I have already stated in a previous chapter, some researchers have theorized that the pineal gland is responsible for paranormal abilities and is the human neurological radar device, abnormally shaped in the brains of those with a propensity towards paranormal or psychic skills. It is surrounded by minute crystalline deposits that radiate magnetic waves enabling the individual to psychically 'home in' to the supersensual areas of the universe. As I have previous stated, the pineal gland is larger in a child than in the adult, and marginally more developed in the female than in the male. This is probably the reason why a high percentage of children have paranormal experiences; for example, seeing things nobody else can see, and why women are generally speaking far more psychically aware than men.

Nostradamus and Herbal Narcotic

Before the seer Nostradamus obtained his prophetic visions, he would imbibe a herbal narcotic, the contents of which were known to him alone. This would induce a hypnotic trance-like state, during which Nostradamus would glean information about future events. Nostradamus was by profession a physician and apothecary, so therefore knew all about hallucinogenic compounds and the effects they have upon the brain. Nostradamus was not alone in the use of hallucinogenic concoctions, as many secret spiritual organizations at the time relied upon them to obtain information that was only accessible through transcendental means.

Effects on the Brain

Hallucinogens somehow bypass neurological space and time, allowing the user to completely lose sense of both and to enter a euphoric transcendental state, during which sensory perception is heightened. Time is not a material condition but is a product of human consciousness. Although the arbitrary nature of time is more obvious when we sleep, simply because we longer have any point of reference to measure it, hallucinogenic substances allow both time and space to be somehow bypassed so it becomes totally under our control. The ancient seers were fully aware of the transcendental nature of time and space and knew exactly how consciousness could be employed as a bridge with which to transcend the transitory elements of the external world. Although many of the ancient seers found the use of hallucinogens more than effective, a minority imbibed them for the wrong reasons and were seen to prostitute their abilities by gaining control of their ignorant devotees. Some even abused the sacred hallucinogens to such an extent that the psychological effects on them were irreversible and they eventually went insane.

Of course the use of hallucinogenic compounds was not the only method ancient priests would employ to induce transcendental states of consciousness. The much safer methods of various techniques of meditation were also used to heighten the awareness, and to induce trance-like states of consciousness. Many priests would also use scrying techniques to bring about altered states of awareness. By focusing the attention on a bowl of water or even a crystal speculum, a self-induced trance-like state could be quickly brought about.

Meditation

Deep meditation can also enable the practitioner to lose all notion of time, simply because any mental activity is situated on the subconscious level. It can be said that time, as we usually conceive it, is an objective state of consciousness. From the very moment we transcend that state and pass the limits of conscious objectivity, we lose all sense of duration. That is exactly what happens when we sleep or when, for any other reason, we are no longer conscious of our earthly surroundings, as in the case when we have been anaesthetized in preparation for surgery. The Shaman priests were fully aware of these altered states of consciousness, which they would induce either through hallucinogens or meditative practices. The hallucinogenic compound, psilocybin, extracted from the sacred mushroom, was also favored by Aztec and Shamanic priests. Once this had been imbibed it would produce another hallucinogenic compound in the body called psilocin, the chemical formula of which is $C_{12} H_{16} N_2O$.

Science and Illusory Effect

Some scientists have even suggested that paranormal experiences are merely the illusory effects of a chemical imbalance in the brain, rather like the neurological phenomenon induced by hallucinogenic compounds. This suggests then that nothing really tangible exists beyond the confines of the mind. This more or less concurs with the Buddhist theory that the external world is an illusion (Maya) and that the only reality is produced by the mind.

Pranayama and Transcendental Experience

From time immemorial man has sought ways of achieving a transcendental experience, either with the use of hallucinogenic compounds, deep meditation or even through various breathing techniques the yogi masters referred to as Pranayama, roughly translated as the control of *prana*. The yogic concept of breath control has been employed for thousands of years as a means of promoting higher states of consciousness. It is the yogic belief that by controlling the inhalations and exhalations of breath it is possible to infuse the body with more pranic energy, thus inducing euphoric or higher states of awareness. Prana is the name they use to describe *all* energy in the universe. It is believed to be the subtle agent through which the life of the body is sustained. The yogic masters teach that the quality of life is greatly affected through the respiratory process of drawing in and maintaining higher levels of prana in the body, and that by suspending the breath one is able to control the effects of time on the physiological and psychological processes, thus ensuring longevity. Although prana is in the air we breathe, it is not the air itself; while it is not matter, prana is contained in all forms of matter. The animal and the plant kingdoms take prana in with the air, and should it not be present with each breath, death would occur. So, we now have a good idea that prana has its own particular parts to play in the manifestation of life, apart from the obvious physiological functions. Once again we can clearly see that the mind is the common denominator, and that consciousness may be precipitated with the use of certain disciplines and practices.

Scrying

Another example is the ancient practice of scrying, particularly with the crystal speculum. The crystal speculum has been used for thousands of years as a means of gleaning information about the future. The actual process involved in scrying is to self-induce a hypnotic state. The practitioner simply gazed at a specific point on the crystal speculum, ensuring that he or she resisted the temptation to blink or move the eyes away even for a single moment. After a few moments the crystal speculum would have the appearance of coming 'alive' and would appear to move. This phenomenon would be followed by a descending shadow that would remain across the crystal speculum for a few moments longer. The shadow would eventually rise to reveal glowing images such as landscapes and anonymous faces, which the seer would interpret. Although the process of crystal gazing sounds quite easy, the skill actually took many years to cultivate and perfect. The crystal speculum was and still is only used as a focal point for the concentration, and the images that appear are not actually in the crystal speculum itself, but are reflected on the image-making faculty of the brain. And so the mind is truly capable of great transcendental achievements and is the portal to many dimensions.

Chapter Eighteen

The Process of Psychic Development

I freely admit that I am guilty, along with many others, of conducting workshops specifically for those endeavoring to develop their psychic and mediumistic abilities. In fact, today we appear to have gone workshop crazy with the devotees of the paranormal enthusiastically seeking knowledgeable teachers to show them how to cultivate their psychic skills. There appears to be far more mediums today than there were even 20 years ago. There are mediums galore demonstrating their mediumistic abilities in theaters, hotels and halls all over the UK. As America is usually well ahead of us where psychics and clairvoyants are concerned, I'm quite certain that it's the same in the USA. However, they can't all be genuine mediums, can they? After all, although everyone possesses psychic abilities potentially, to some greater or lesser degree, the same process does not apply to mediums. In fact, as I have affirmed in an earlier chapter, mediums are born and not made! Contrary to popular belief, a mediumistic ability can only be developed where the potential is already present, and no techniques can cultivate something that is simply not there. Psychic abilities are completely different. It has been suggested that before our prehistoric forebears evolved even the most rudimentary form of speech that they communi-cated their thoughts and feelings telepathically. One notable writer Maurice Maeterlinck once said, "Man only developed speech so that he could tell lies!" Whether or not the latter indictment is true, the fact is the whole process of mediumship is based on telepathy – that is mind-to-mind communication – an incarnate mind to a discarnate mind. A psychic skill maybe defined as a heightened intuitive skill and nothing more.

Intuition

In fact, I always use the word *Intuition* as an umbrella term to cover the whole spectrum of mental abilities. Intuition is one skill we all have in common to some greater or lesser degree; even though it is more highly attuned in some people than others. Intuition may be described as our inherent prehistoric warning device that enables us to simply 'know' things. A police officer who is extremely good at his or her job is very often highly intuitive, as is a doctor who can accurately assess a sick patient before any procedural tests are carried out.

Automatic Pilot

Intuition is also closely connected to the mechanism frequently referred to as the 'automatic pilot', a neurological process that takes us from *A* to *B* without any conscious intervention. In fact, we frequently experience the process of automatic pilot at different levels during the course of the day. For example, you may have been driving home through the rush-hour traffic, your mind processing the day's events at the office and completely unaware of the journey. Before you know it you are parked in the driveway of your home with no recollection of the journey from work having been made. Although a simple example, it illustrates perfectly well the way automatic pilot actually works at a mental level. In fact, psychologically the human *Intellect* and the *Instinctive Mind* are closely associated in the neurological processing of data. When you're learning a new task and you are totally engrossed with it, your mental skills are functioning at the intellectual level while it is processing the task at hand. Once you have mastered whatever it is you are endeavoring to learn, it is then passed down to the instinctive level where it is then processed automatically without even thinking about it. Once again this is a crude analogy but one that perfectly illustrates the mental processing system of absorbing unfamiliar information.

The Intellect also represents the 'I' consciousness in the

average man. On one side of *Intellect* there is 'Spiritual Mind', the reservoir of all inspiration, and on the other side of Intellect there is 'Instinctive Mind', sending the intellect all the old impulses and habits and trying desperately to pull it down and prevent it from evolving. Spiritual Mind does not in any way run contrary to the Intellect; it simply goes beyond the Intellect. It passes down to the Intellect certain truths which it finds in its own regions of the mind, and the Intellect reasons about them. Spiritual truths do not originate with Intellect; Intellect is cold, and Spiritual Mind is warm and alive with high feelings. Individuals who live out their lives totally at an intellectual level, such as academics, tend on the whole to be extremely analytical and very blinkered, at least where spiritual matters are concerned. Occasionally the impulses from Spiritual Mind manage to filter through to the Intellect and then he or she experiences a flash of inspiration. This is very often all that is needed for the individual to discard the blinkers and encourage the Intellect to explore the new horizons of Spiritual Mind. In the cultivation of psychic or spiritual abilities the aspirant needs to be at least open to the impulses of Spiritual Mind and allow the Intellect to diligently process what it receives. Access to Spiritual Mind is spontaneous and is not a process that occurs simply by wanting it to. The spontaneity of Spiritual Mind is primarily dependent upon the individual's expanding awareness, very often precipitated through meditation and self-analysis. The degree of psychic ability attained is solely dependent upon the potential already present in the individual. Although this potential is usually present when the individual is born, it atrophies with lack of use. Psychic development is primarily the ability to remember what has been forgotten, rather than the development of something new. Or, to put it another way, *psychic development is not a process of receiving as much as it is a process of remembering*. The process of mediumistic development works very much in the same, only in my opinion mediumistic potential is only in a minority of people. As I have already affirmed, mediums are born and not made! And no amount of exercises will develop a mediumistic ability where the potential is not already present. Just as the physical body can be exercised to increase its muscle tone and power, so too can the mind be exercised to improve its efficiency and performance. Meditation is the key to self-mastery and has been used for thousands of years as a means of attaining higher states of consciousness. However, what meditation technique is suitable for one person may not necessarily be suitable for another. Not everyone has the patience or the ability to concentrate for any length of time, and so the individual needs to be holistically considered when creating the appropriate meditation technique.

The Maharishi and TM

Meditation itself takes many forms, from simple scrying techniques, to the more complicated systems consisting of various mental exercises. In the 1960s, Indian physicist the Maharishi Mahesh Yogi devised an effective system of meditation he called Transcendental Meditation, or TM for short. This was popularized by the Beatles when they became devotees of the Maharishi. This was all that was needed to launch Transcendental Meditation on to the world. TM centers opened worldwide, and Transcendental Meditation was revered as the meditation that would alleviate the stresses of living in the modern age. The practitioners of TM were given a personal mantra for them to use, with the instruction that it was to be repeated over and over for the maximum effect to be achieved.

Chanting Mantras

Transcendental Meditation was in fact a modified version of an ancient yogic system that involved chanting. There are numerous mantras that may be used in meditation, from the well-known *OM or AUM*, to the *OM MANI PADME AUM*, the Jewel in the

Lotus. The psychological and emotional effects of meditation are quite remarkable, which is why it is prescribed by many general practitioners to help their patients cope with stress and anxiety.

Meditation encourages the release of endorphins in the brain, the body's natural painkillers that also produce feelings of euphoria. Apart from the physiological and psychological effects of meditation, it is also known to encourage changes in the electrical circuitry of the brain and nerve centers by affecting movement of energy through the seven major centers known as 'Chakras'. Although the Eastern concept of energy is comparatively new to the Western way of thinking, with new technology numerous sophisticated devices are now available to enable the movement of subtle energy throughout the body to be monitored, and also the precise location of the seven vortices known as chakras. This technology now confirms what has been taught in Eastern esoteric traditions for thousands of years, and substantiates the suggestion that carefully integrated into the human organism is a subtle, more spiritualized part of man's being.

There is undoubtedly something quite intrinsic in human psychology that makes one person believe in mediums and all things paranormal, and makes another person dismiss it completely. Whatever this 'thing' is, it is also present in the psychological makeup of the individuals who desperately feel that they possess some sort of mediumistic ability when they do not! After all, how can you believe in ghosts when you have never seen one? How can you believe that such things as mediumistic skills exist when you have never experienced them?

Chapter Nineteen

The Facts About Some Mediums

I have known and indeed worked with hundreds of mediums over the years, and have also employed clairvoyants I did not really know to do some events I had organized in various parts of the North of England. Apart from the ones with whom I have worked closely, my observations of some of them led me to believe that they all work in the same way, and their abilities would not in any way stand up to close scrutiny. Some years ago now I put on a special evening for Everton Football Club, for which I had to engage 20 clairvoyants. These consisted of tarot readers, palmists and mediums of all different kinds. The event was a 'Psychic Supper', during which everyone would have a meal and a short reading with a clairvoyant. Tables of ten were laid out in the main function room and a clairvoyant placed at each one. After the meal had been eaten the clairvoyant would commence giving each person a short message. I had been putting these events on for Everton Football Club for some years and they had always proven to be extremely popular, particularly around Halloween. Although there was always someone who would make a complaint, usually that the reading had not been long enough, the majority of people were usually very pleased. On this particular evening I engaged the services of a medium from Blackburn, a gentleman who shall remain nameless for obvious reasons. I'd never met him before, and those who did know him warned me that he was awful. I do believe in giving everyone a chance, and anyway I had to see him work for myself. As it transpired, he had finished his table long before anyone else and came to me for his fee. As he was waiting the whole of his table confronted me, each complaining about him. He had apparently given them all more or less the same reading, and had done so before the meal and not after as he was supposed to do. He had obviously pre-empted what was happening, and before I could confront him with the angry women, he had made a hasty retreat, climbed into his car and had gone home, without his fee.

Another medium I used on my stage shows, primarily because of the way the audience warmed towards her, always appeared to give the same messages on every show. The woman in question was a diabetic and so you could be certain that at least two people in the audience would be told that somebody had died with diabetes. "I know this," she would always add, "because my mouth always goes dry!" Yeah, right! As I have previously said, all mediums (myself included) use 'fillers', to make the delivery of the messages more interesting. But this medium appeared to have a different list of messages for each theater. I became suspicious when I received several complaints at a local theater. Frequently a medium will get away with an awful lot simply because of his or her warmth and the way they manipulate an audience. Stagecraft, presentation and style are everything when demonstrating mediumistic skills in a theater. This is far different to demonstrating in a Spiritualist Church.

Mediums Being Scrutinized

Although I cannot mention anybody by name, two high profile television mediums are being discretely investigated because of the way it is believed they obtain information about members of their audiences. One particular medium gets theater audiences to fill in a questionnaire before the show, stating who they have lost, his or her name and how they died! These questionnaires are then passed to the medium in question who then randomly selects one at a time. Of course, the recipient of the message very often feels either intimidated because he or she has to stand up while they are given the message, or are far too polite to say anything. Of course, to the majority of the audience the medium's demonstration is impressive. However, as we now know, the general public is becoming more discerning where mediums are concerned, and many members of this particular medium's audiences are now becoming increasingly more suspicious.

Stage Mediums

Although stage mediums are frequently accused of getting up to all sorts of antics to obtain information about members of an audience, such as obtaining credit card details etc, generally speaking they now use more sophisticated ways to ensure their shows are successful. Another medium, who again shall remain nameless, before his popular television program enlisted the help of people to interview selected members of the studio audience. The information obtained is then given to the medium who then has prior knowledge about selected members of the television audience. The viewer at home only see an impressive performance, and so the medium's popularity grows even more.

Maltese Television

I am very aware just how a television program can be edited to make a medium look extremely impressive. Alternatively it can be edited to make the medium look anything but impressive. In 2002 I appeared on a television program in Malta. This was a magazine program called *Xarabank*, and although at the time I had no idea what sort of program it was, I was soon to discover that it was an extremely popular controversial program that investigated different topics. I was to demonstrate my mediumistic skills before a studio audience of 200 Catholics. I demonstrated my skills for nearly five hours with only a few minute's break every forty minutes. Fortunately for me the demonstration went extremely well, with me relaying messages from the deceased relatives of selected members of the audience. This was on the Wednesday, and on the Friday I had to be questioned by an exorcist priest and a Catholic psychologist. The producers expected the audience to return on the Friday to criticize my mediumistic demonstration, and the panel were prepared to join in. However, to everyone's surprise all those who had received messages returned with photographs of the deceased relatives from whom they had received messages. Everyone was there to support and not condemn me. However, the producers were prepared for this and not only showed the recording of the positive side of my demonstration, but also showed how it could be edited to discredit me. Luckily the audience supported me and even spoke up in my defense. The producer asked the Catholic priest, "Father, how did Billy Roberts do this?" To which came the expected and very obvious reply, "I don't know, but he is working with the devil!" My appearance on *Xarabank* apparently attracted the highest viewing figures for a long time and left the producer (himself a devout skeptic) scratching his head. My appearance on Maltese television made me realize just how vulnerable mediums actually are when appearing on such programs, and just how easy it is for the media to damage a medium's career forever. However, I think it was journalist, Hannen Swaffer who once said, "No publicity is bad!" I'm not too certain that that's entirely true, but some mediums have proven this to be the case.

Dr. Ciarán O'Keeffe and Acorah

Celebrity medium, Derek Acorah frequently fell into 'trance' on the popular television program *Most Haunted*. Having become suspicious of Acorah's antics, Dr. Ciarán O'Keeffe the program's resident parapsychologist decided to set about exposing him and his alleged trance. He created a couple of anagrams using 'Derek the faker' which read 'Kreed Kafer'. The anagram was fed to Derek Acorah as being the name of a person who once resided in the property in which the program was being filmed. The medium fell for it hook, line and sinker! While in 'trance' he was asked what his name was. "Kreed Kafer," was the reply. "Kreed Kafer!" Although other attempts to expose Acorah were in fact made by Dr. O'Keeffe, the medium was virtually untouched by the bad publicity and in fact went from strength to strength, and today still appears regularly on television. I do have to say that Dr. Ciarán O'Keeffe's exposé does not in itself mean that Derek Acorah is not genuine; it simply indicates that the one incident was not a true demonstration of trance mediumship.

Doris Stokes

When a medium has reached certain heights in his or her profession, his or her popularity status has to be maintained, very often at any cost. Sometimes this is done quite innocently to ensure positive results in the show. Before Doris Stokes died I was asked to compére one of her shows in Sheffield. I spent the afternoon with Doris and her manager Laurie O'Leary in her hotel. At the time Doris was waiting to go into hospital for neurological surgery, and so I knew she wasn't in the best of health. While I enjoyed my lunch I overheard her manager briefing her about some of the audience guests. He reminded her that the names he had mentioned to her were also mentioned in one of her books. I was quite surprised to hear him tell her that if she encountered any difficulties with her messages during the show that she should call upon the names he had given her. The show began in the usual way with Doris explaining to the audience what she was going to do, and then she proceeded to relay messages to selected members of the audience. I noticed that the first messages were somewhat ambiguous and I could see she was struggling. I was completely surprised when she called out the name Paul Strachan. A young man put his hand up and was promptly ushered to the stage. Doris then proceeded to relay to the young man everything she had been told in her hotel room that day. The following message involved a woman whose Australian brother had been killed in suspicious circumstances.

Once again, something she had been told by her manager during the day. Of course, Doris only gave approximately three messages that she had been told about by her manager during the afternoon, and there were many other genuinely acquired messages relayed to selected members of a very happy audience. Needless to say, Doris Stokes did not recover from her surgery but passed away in hospital some weeks later. So-called high profile mediums do have a responsibility to their audiences and do have to maintain their standard in order to sustain their popularity. Even when demonstrating on television, one can never know what preparations have occurred before the show to ensure a good program. After all, the viewer ratings are really all that matter when demonstrating mediumistic skills on a television program. I am not suggesting for one moment that all mediums are a party to this sort of 'cheating', but I am quite sure that the general public now know only too well that it does occasionally occur. Although Victorian mediums were notorious for employing 'cheating' techniques to dupe their audiences, today people are far more educated about mediumistic practices, and are fully aware of the tricks some mediums get up to. In saying this, mediums are damned if they do and damned if they don't. They are in a no-win situation where their mediumistic abilities are concerned. If they give an excellent and genuine demonstration of mediumistic skills, they are accused of cheating, and they are criticized if their demonstration is poor. Who would want the hassle of being a medium?

Chapter Twenty

Methods of Communication and Psychology

It is really now quite difficult to believe that the Ouija board was once sold in toy shops, and that such a method of divination once fascinated and amused children worldwide. The manufacturer of the bizarre toy, Waddington, also made the board game Monopoly, and such was the interest in their Ouija board that it was extremely popular and was sold right up until the early 1960s. Then, there were very stern warnings about the Ouija board and the dangers that may result in its use. Experts in the paranormal warned that the Ouija board attracted negative energies and could psychologically affect anyone who played around with it. In fact, many users of the Ouija board had awful experiences and believed that they were possessed by evil spirits. Other people believed that after they used the Ouija board they were plagued with bad luck.

Psychology

The more scientifically minded dismissed the Ouija board as no more than an object of amusement, primarily affected by ideomotor action, involuntary and unconscious motor behavior, rather than movement affected by external forces. The term ideomotor action was coined by William Benjamin Carpenter in 1852 who suggested that users of the Ouija board caused the pointer to move with the involuntary or even subconscious movement of the muscles. Regardless of what the scientifically minded suggest about the Ouija board, it is my opinion that there is very little doubt that some forms of disembodied intelligences are involved in the process of communication through it. It is also quite clear that these intelligences are nearly always of a low spiritual order, regardless of the content and quality of the information gleaned. The Ouija board should not be taken lightly and should never, ever be used as a form of amusement. If it is to be used at all it is always advisable to be supervised by a medium or someone equally qualified to do so.

The Planchette and Psychology

The planchette is another device greatly favored by Victorian Spiritualists. This was a very simple moveable device that held a writing implement such as a pencil, usually on a small ball to allow it freedom of movement. The user simply placed a finger gently on the device while mentally preoccupying himself, usually reading a book, so as to eliminate the possibility of consciously interfering with the writing process. The planchette would move across the blank piece of paper, scratching out the writing of a disembodied person. Again scientists and parapsychologists suggest that the writing process involves a little subconscious action, even though the user is elsewhere preoccupied. For every genuine Victorian medium there were at least ten fake mediums, each one extremely proficient in the art of séance fabrication.

The Parlor Séance and the Trumpet

The séance trumpet was a prime example of séance chicanery, and the majority of those who perpetrated the heinous act had no qualms whatsoever about what they were doing. They were usually paid handsomely for the demonstrations of trickery, and the Victorians were so fascinated by mediums and the so-called 'parlor séance' that they were prepared to pay anything to sit with a medium. The aluminum trumpet would be placed on the table, around which would sit the expectant recipients of messages. The mediums always insisted on the room being in total darkness, and to ensure no light at all filtered in from the gas-lit lampposts in the street outside, heavy drapes would be drawn across the windows. A few moments would elapse while the medium prepared himself and to allow the luminous strip on the aluminum trumpet to become visible. The medium would make a few grunting sounds as his head swayed from side to side and he slipped gently into a trance-like swoon. Of course, all the sitters were so enthralled by the whole ambience it rarely occurred to any of them that trickery was afoot.

A further few minutes would elapse before the trumpet would rise into the air, seemingly lifted by a disembodied hand. It occasionally moved round the table at some great speed before stopping in front of one of the expectant séance attendees. A disembodied voice would boom from the trumpet, purporting to be that of a deceased husband or wife. The voice very often sounded nothing whatsoever like the person it was supposed to be, but by now the recipient of the message was so excited that he or she nearly always happily responded. Although not all séance demonstrations were faked, the ones that were fabricated were carried out in an extremely sophisticated and very professional way. The sitters would be unaware that the medium was actually on his knees by now and manually moving the trumpet around the circle himself. Occasionally someone would become suspicious and turn on the lights. Even then, however, the medium would nearly always come up with some feeble excuse to explain exactly why he was on his hands and knees. The favored excuses were either that "I was in trance; I did not know what I was doing!" Or "My Spirit Guide occasionally does this to me!" And so it goes on. I am of course only talking about the 'fake' séances, as I'm sure you probably know that there were many very genuine ones at that time.

Table Tipping

The levitating table was another favorite trick, although for obvious reasons this fabrication could only be perpetrated in the medium's own home. The medium would wear a ring with a small hook attached to it. This hook would correspond with a similar one neatly concealed at the edge of the table. The medium usually had a friend working with him on the far side of the table. He or she would also have a ring with a concealed hook attached. All the sitters would be instructed to place their hands gently on the table, completely unaware that the two charlatans had carefully connected the hooks on their rings to the table. Lo and behold! To everyone's amazement the heavy table would rise from the floor. Table tipping became every Victorian medium's favorite party piece, and few actually became suspicious of exactly how the trick was performed. Of course there were many different sophisticated ways of duping the unsuspecting audiences, as I am sure there are today.

Even though fake mediums were still very much in evidence, the very early part of the twentieth century saw the advent of psychical research groups and so fake mediums became more cautious and a little less daring in the things they got up to. Today those interested in the paranormal are in the main more discerning and know exactly what to look out for when exploring mediums and the different kinds of phenomena.

Today, as in Victorian times, the messages relayed to selected members of a congregation or audience are nearly always ambiguous with either no names at all given to the recipient, or a lot of first names with an occasional surname, which is very rarely accepted. Although the general public are nearly always willing to accept even the vaguest of messages from a medium, once he or she has had sufficient time to think about and digest the information they have been given, they usually see it in a completely different light. As I have previously stated, mediums are in a no-win situation, and are damned if they don't and damned if they do! It was never my intention to decry or dismiss all mediums as fakes, but more to highlight the growing problem of the not so genuine medium. It is far too easy to set up as a working medium or clairvoyant, and until the laws regarding mediums change dramatically the problem will continue to grow.

Chapter Twenty-One

Bad Skeptics

If I am to explore the psychology of a medium, then it is only fair that I should also make a detailed analysis of the psychology of a skeptic. I am not just referring to the person who simply does not believe; I am talking about the skeptic who goes all out to publicly have his or her say, to the extent of setting up a group of like-minded skeptics, perhaps even with an Internet forum where other skeptics can have their say. What is it that makes this sort of skeptic feel they have a mission to decry mediums and all things paranormal? Usually their skepticism is based on one or perhaps two experiences with mediums. Or they may even make an assessment on the mediums they have seen on television. I am the first to admit that not all mediums and clairvoyants are genuine, and many of the ones who are genuine are perhaps not the best ambassadors for the mediumistic profession. However, the majority of so-called skeptics I have encountered are skeptical just for the sake of it. It has been some years now since I have done a theater show, or for that matter anything in the North of England, and yet some skeptics (some of them not old enough to have seen me) still criticize and dismiss my mediumship. These attacks are frequently perpetrated on many mediums and are obviously done for the sake of it. But what is a skeptic really? Well, strictly speaking a skeptic is from the ancient Greek school of philosophy, the members of which proclaim that real knowledge is impossible! It is a fact that one can only attain knowledge of a subject by making a study of it. The majority of skeptics do not even consider this and prefer to dismiss mediumistic and paranormal skills completely. This inane attitude does not in any way do skeptics any favors, and to claim (as some do) that nobody is capable of receiving communication from the so-called 'dead' without investigating it is unintelligent in itself. I am not suggesting that ALL skeptics are unintelligent; far from it! Many skeptics are academics, doctors, university lecturers, who really should know better. Everyone is allowed an opinion, and we thankfully live in a nation where we are allowed freedom of speech, thank God! Oh, there I go again, thanking God when we don't really know if he/she exists. We all do it several times a day, when our belief in God is more based on faith than it is on fact. Even though there is no tangible evidence for the existence of God it does not stop us mentioning his name in general conversation several times a day, does it? Even skeptics will frequently say, "Thank God" or even "God knows!" In fact, I have had many a heated conversation with a skeptic, and from the very beginning of the debate I realized that I was in a no-win situation. However, after affirming that the paranormal and mediums were rubbish, the skeptic thoughtfully announced, "But there was this one time when I saw... " So, it would appear that even skeptics have a story to tell! I can understand someone being skeptical of the paranormal and mediums in particular, but what I can't understand is why they have to carry a skeptic's banner and shout it from the rooftops! Saint Paul was a bigoted skeptic, but even he was eventually converted, albeit by the hard evidence. Skeptics just need to be vigilant, and wait and see what transpires during their quest to disprove anyone with paranormal skills. Over the years I have become known as a skeptical medium, simply because I have to see it to believe it. I have seen hundreds, maybe thousands of mediums demonstrating their mediumistic skills, and it is really only a minority who have given me a message that has truly convinced me that they were genuine. It doesn't matter how accurate a message appears when it is given to another person; it is only when it is given to you can you confirm and validate its accuracy. To many mediums it is an easy way of making money, to a minority it is a vocation. Skeptics accuse all mediums of exploiting the weak and vulnerable, and also say that if a medium is genuine he or she would not charge for their services. That may well be the skeptic's opinion, but if a medium does nothing else but demonstrate mediumistic skills then who feeds them, and pays their rent or mortgage? To enable a medium to devote his or her life to their work they need to be paid for their services, just like anyone else. One could say the same about a vicar or a priest; but they too receive some remuneration from the church. Mediums pay their taxes just like anyone else who does a job of work.

Completely Dismissing the Paranormal

Open-minded skepticism is the healthy way to approach the paranormal, as opposed to dismissing it completely without consideration as 'rubbish!' Open-minded skepticism is to devout skepticism what agnosticism is to atheism. One so-called 'skeptic' introduced himself to me as a 'paranormal agnostic!' That description makes more sense to me and is a far more acceptable term. In fact, until you have discovered the real hard evidence, then I believe that everyone should be a paranormal agnostic. To dismiss the paranormal or mediumistic skills without any consideration is inane and unintelligent. I can appreciate someone being a devout skeptic on the basis that he or she has had a bad experience with a medium, or in fact knows someone whose vulnerability has been exploited by a bad medium. But even then one should explore all the possibilities for themselves. Anecdotal evidence is very unreliable and personal experience is the only way to reach a final positive conclusion. Today it seems to be just as fashionable to be a skeptic as it is to be involved in the paranormal. I have already stated in an earlier chapter that mediums now need more than a reliable skill if they are to stand up to the more academically qualified skeptic. Mediums also require knowledge and a deeper understanding of their craft to enable them to meet the skeptic head on in any confrontational situation. I co-authored *The Great Paranormal Clash* with parapsychologist Dr. Ciarán O'Keeffe. Our two very different perspectives gave us the basis for a stage show of the same name. Interest in this has been overwhelming, as it gives the audience the opportunity to listen to two very different viewpoints of the paranormal and mediums. During the stage show Dr. O'Keeffe endeavors to show the audience exactly how he believes mediums do what they do, using 'cold reading' techniques and other psychological methods. It is my job of course to demonstrate my mediumistic skills to selected members of the audience, taking great care to avoid relaying vague and ambiguous messages that could be described as the 'Barnum effect' – that is a message that is given to one person and yet could apply to any member of the audience. The primary purpose of *The Great Paranormal Clash* is to educate the devotees of the paranormal as to its implications and realities, and is open to skeptics and believers alike.

Chapter Twenty-Two

Stone Tape Phenomenon

Russian researchers have concluded that we possess a bioplasmic body as well as other subtle vehicles, and that we appear to constantly discharge particles of bioplasma all through our lives. It has been suggested that these discharged particles gradually impregnate the surrounding atmosphere and are taken up by the subtle structure of the bricks and mortar of the places we inhabit. And so it would appear that we are constantly leaving behind particles of ourselves everywhere we go, contributing to the construction of the subtle atmosphere of the environment in which we live. It has been suggested that this bioplasmic atmosphere serves as a sort of subtle screen upon which images and sounds of past events are captured. Just as audio and video tapes are coated with minute particles of an electromagnetic substance, enabling them to capture sounds and images, it would appear that so too is the subtle atmosphere impregnated with the same electromagnetic materials. Water appears to be an extremely effective conduit for paranormal activity, which old, damp bricks and mortar structures retain, maintaining the energies of the past. Although the majority of sensitive individuals have no difficulty whatsoever accessing these, even the non-psychically inclined person can experience these without any difficulty at all.

Photographic Image

The majority of so-called apparitions are no more than photo-graphic images from the past, and possess no intelligence or conscious awareness of the present time. When these sorts of apparitions do make an appearance, the sounds that usually accompany them are very rarely synchronized to the paranormal manifestation itself, and are usually just a cacophony of unrelated eerie, spine chilling noises. I am not suggesting that there are no genuine paranormal visitations. On the contrary, I am merely stating that the majority of what are perceived as a spirit manifestations are no more than occurrences of bioplasmic energy with natural and very logical explanations. This phenomenon is sometimes referred to as the 'stone tape' phenomenon and is the production of paranormal phenomena caused by a very natural occurrence. I have already mentioned that some paranormal activity is occasionally produced by the geological phenomenon referred to as Triboluminescence. This phenomenon is produced by friction of crystals or other mineral deposits below ground level. Activity produced by triboluminescence interrupts the electromagnetic atmosphere and very often precipitates paranormal activity. The geological phenomenon can also interrupt the electrical circuitry of the brains of certain individuals causing psychic or transcendental experiences. As I said in an earlier chapter, sufferers of temporal lobe epilepsy are especially susceptible to the influencing activity of triboluminescence, which appears to cause a temporary interruption in the person's cognitive response mechanism. Whether an apparition is the result of natural occurrences or a disembodied visitation is irrelevant to the individual who encounters it alone in the dead of night! Both manifestations give rise to the natural responses of the brain, and from then on the imagination takes over. If a person is told that he or she is being taken in the dead of night to an alleged haunted location, long before the destination has been reached the mind will have already created its own ghosts and demons. The mind controls the automatic reactions of the imagination, and together they affect the visual and response mechanism making appear very real what is not really there! As it is all a matter of perception where paranormal phenomena are concerned, the mind is the common denominator when endeavoring to make a rational assessment of paranormal experiences. Einstein once said, "the is only one thing more important than knowledge, and that is imagination." Imagination is what makes us who and what we are, and is an extremely important faculty when one is involved in the paranormal.

In my experience of haunted locations I can honestly say that in 30 years of paranormal investigations I have never found a consistency in paranormal activity at any one particular location. Even the paranormal occurrences at the most popular locations do not appear to be consistent, and long periods of time can elapse before a paranormal occurrence. Many of the 'ghost hunting' programs on television nearly always capture some form of audio or visual paranormal phenomena, but very often contribute every commonplace sound to a disembodied source. With all the sophisticated paranormal equipment at our disposal today, I would expect to witness much more than a few knocking sounds or even an unusual light anomaly, both of which can have a logical explanation. Even ghostly apparitions caught on camera are nearly always indistinct with deliberate repetitive movements, indicating that it is more the photographic image phenomenon as opposed to a genuine discarnate apparition. The house in which I live is a sixteenth century farmhouse, which is also an integral part of a complex of converted barns and other very old dwellings. Before the previous owner knew what I did for a living he warned my wife and I that the house was very haunted. In fact, it is common knowledge throughout the community that Pool House is haunted and is the home to several ghosts. One ghostly inhabitant was a chambermaid sometime in the eighteenth century. The previous owner's daughters allegedly found out that her name was Dorothy via a Ouija board, and they were told in no uncertain terms that she disliked Christmas. She apparently demonstrated her displeasure by causing Christmas cards and other decorations to fly across the room from their place on the mantel. Although at the time of writing this book we have not as yet had a Christmas in our new home, my wife and I have both seen Dorothy, a tall rather distinguished looking woman in her mid-fifties, making her way from the cellar and disappearing through the downstairs toilet door. As she followed the same route day in and day out, always at around 3.30 in the afternoon, I was totally confused. However, I later found out from the previous owner that there used to be a door where the toilet is now and our house and the house next door used to be one dwelling. I first thought that as Dorothy followed the same route all the time that she was just a photographic memory; until, that is, she turned and smiled at me as I was working at my computer. It is now nearing the end of October and as my wife and I both love Christmas, we are hoping that we can convert Dorothy's dislike of Christmas into joy. Apart from the ghostly apparition of Dorothy, we frequently see a mass of colored mist moving around the bedroom. This usually dissipates after several minutes, culminating into a display of light anomalies gyrating across the ceiling. There is no doubt about it, our new home has certainly helped to change my views about many visual and audible paranormal phenomena. What we have experienced in this house has been mostly objective paranormal phenomena and has been witnessed on many occasions by my wife, and has no connection with the fact that I am mediumistically inclined. Although I have always been suspicious of knocking sounds where paranormal phenomena are concerned, there are very unusual knocking and bumping sounds in our house that definitely suggest some form of rudimentary intelligence. By this I mean that whoever is behind the phenomena responds to my request each time to repeat the knocking. The house is two-stories high and we sleep in the uppermost apex of what was once-upon-a-time the attic. As with all old houses, the stairs are very creaky and in the dead of night, usually around 3am, we both wake up to the sound of creaking and footsteps coming up the stairs. Our two pussycats Elly and Poppy also wake up at 3am and watch the bedroom door intently, as though expecting to see it to open at any minute and someone to walk into the room. We've become quite accustomed to the bumps, knocks and groans, although I have always wondered what the purpose to the knocking sounds actually is! In themselves they seem pretty pointless, even though they do contribute something to the whole cacophony of spooky sounds.

Overall, there has to be some form of intelligence (albeit rudimentary) behind the majority of paranormal phenomena as they nearly always respond when you ask them to stop making the noises. One can understand how the now clichéd 'knock once for yes and twice for no', came about. It has been suggested that the disembodied perpetrators of knockings and wrappings are no longer in possession of a physical body, and that they use the only method they know to communicate with the living. Of course, this very crude method of communication only applies to those with a rudimentary form of intelligence, as those with a more developed mind are able to communicate in a variety of ways. Some experts in the field of metaphysics have also suggested that not all discarnate souls have the ability to actually make their presence visibly known, and that here again it is purely a matter of intelligence and awareness. The disembodied have to acclimatize themselves to the environment in which they live, and it may take some time for him or her to make their presence felt and affect a so-called 'haunting'. There is more than likely an extremely technical side to an actual 'haunting', at least from the perpetrator's point of view. I don't think for one moment that paranormal activity is affected just by the discarnate actually being there! There has to be some intention behind a real haunting, with quite a lot of energy expended on the part of the discarnate presence. Once the disembodied presence has caught the attention of the inhabitants of the dwelling it wishes to haunt, its energy and power is somehow increased giving the entity greater focus and control of its activity. In my experience there are many different types of paranormal activity, and only a minority of these are the results of actual disembodied energies.

Chapter Twenty-Three

Mechanics of Mediumship

I have already previously established that the actual process of mediumship is not normal, inasmuch as actually seeing so-called 'dead' people is not something that the majority of society would regard as psychologically acceptable. I have also previously stated that mediums are in fact born and not made. By this I mean that the mediumistically inclined individual is genetically predisposed from birth, and the ability is not something that can normally be cultivated in later life simply because the person possesses an overwhelming desire to be a medium. The majority of people have a little understanding of what a medium actually is, but usually equate a mediumistically inclined individual with any psychic or clairvoyant. These assumptions are quite common given the fact that innumerable misconceptions are born from sheer ignorance of the various mediumistic skills. What is generally termed 'mental mediumship' is an umbrella term to cover the mediumistic abilities of clairvoyance, clairaudience and clairsentience. First of all, not all mediums are clairvoyant, and not all clairvoyants are mediums. As you most probably already know clairvoyance simply means 'clear-seeing', and is a term used to describe someone who has the ability to see something the ordinary person cannot. A clairvoyant has the ability to glean things from the future and may occasionally use one of various divinatory devices, such as a crystal ball, tarot cards or even the palm of the sitter's hand. Some clairvoyants do not use anything but their own ability to perceive subjective images, symbols and overwhelming feelings. Images of a deceased person will only become apparent to a clairvoyant if he or she possesses a mediumistic skill, which they will have possessed from birth. As with any ability, psychic or otherwise, there are always varying degrees; but once it becomes apparent it can then be cultivated and developed further. However, even then a skill can only be developed to some greater or lesser degree until the individual's full potential has been achieved. The gift of clairaudience is perhaps one of the lesser-known mediumistic skills. Clairaudience is the term used to describe the gift of 'hearing', and is the rare ability possessed by some mediums enabling them to hear supersensual sounds, usually disembodied voices.

Mediumship and Endocrine System

As all psychic and mediumistic abilities in some way affect the endocrine glands, it is believed that the gift of clairaudience is greatly influenced by the thyroid gland, and many clairaudient mediums in fact suffer with thyroid problems in later life. Clairsentience is perhaps the most common of all mediumistic abilities and is the one that the majority of even non-mediumistically gifted people seem to possess. Clairsentience is the term used to describe the gift of 'clear sensing' and is in some way connected to *intuition*, an ability we all use at some time during the course of the day. Clairsentience is the ability we use when we are alone in the house and think we have heard a noise. Clairsentience causes the hairs on the back of your neck to stand up and goose bumps to appear all over your skin when you are afraid. It is also that part of your heightened awareness that enables you to actually 'sense' an unusual or ghostly presence. The majority of mediums use clairsentience in its heightened form allowing them to glean a broad spectrum of detailed information about a deceased communicator. When a medium is demonstrating his or her abilities, clairaudience nearly always works in tandem with clairvoyance, enabling the medium to give a more detailed piece of information. It is possible for an individual with no mediumistic abilities to possess clairvoyant skills and a rudimentary form of clairaudience and mistakenly believe that he or she is a medium when they are not. This means that fragmented bits of information are always received making the demonstrations of their abilities consistently appear weak, confused and incoherent. This individual is self-deluded and their abilities can therefore never be developed to their full potential, primarily because they are endeavoring to develop something that they just do not possess. Mediumship is quite specific and probably the most unreliable of all paranormal abilities. Although a competent medium can nearly always control his or her mediumistic skills to some degree, because the information that is received through the process of mediumship is frequently inconsistent, it is therefore virtually impossible to bring it fully under control. Mediumship should at the best of times always be considered as an experiment, and even the most competent mediums will have some difficulty in repeating an excellent demonstration of their skills. Therefore, it is unfair to make a judgment about a medium's abilities on the basis that he or she was not too impressive when you first saw them. In my experience all demonstrations of mediumship are different, and a medium is very often only as good as the audience they are working with. The actual mechanics of mediumship does greatly vary from medium to medium, and the results produced during a mediumistic demonstration are very much dependent on the way a medium affects the audience. Some mediums are very adept at manipulating an audience, and without this stagecraft a mediumistic demonstration can prove to be extremely poor and ineffective. As a rule, the audiences of a mediumistic show can be very cruel and some can make it very difficult for a medium to produce an impressive demonstration. The overall psychology of the audience of a psychic show is completely different from that of a medium, as both the individual members of an audience and the mediums who demonstrate to them are frequently endeavoring to achieve two very different things. A medium is very often overwhelmed with the desire to impress the audience, and the majority of those who attend psychic and mediumistic shows are mostly there to assess and make a judgment on the performance and not to massage the medium's ego! The intentions of some mediums are anything but honorable, and many are driven by the very strong desire either to make as much money as possible, or simply to impress, attract a huge following and to become famous. I know many mediums will be appalled at this statement, but over the years I have known and worked with hundreds of very different types of practitioners, and the one thing I have learned is that the majority of them are motivated by ego rather than by the desire to help those in need, regardless of what they say! In recent years I have become increasingly suspicious of mediums who proudly announce that they "work solely for the Spirit World", as is the case with some so-called 'high profile' mediums, whose egos appear to be the only motivating factors. Coming from a professional medium this most probably sounds arrogant and quite cruel, but experience has made me somewhat cynical with an extremely skeptical approach to the entire genre of the paranormal. I have also previously stated that there is no such entity as a healthy genuine medium! The majority of mediums suffer in some way either emotionally or physically. I am quite certain that it is probably a prerequisite for being a medium. Maybe illness makes the medium more compassionate and more sympathetic. Whatever the reason is, a medium's life is not easy, and it would seem that the road a medium walks is always strewn with problems of one kind or another. 'Character building!' my mother always reminded me. I think that sometimes I would prefer to do something completely different, but I know that I never could! There is no doubt at all that there is a very specific psychology to being a medium, and those who choose to embark upon the great adventure of mediumship will find that their lives will never be the same again. Many mediums do suffer from emotional or psychological problems, and in the past 20 years I have known at least 8 mediums who have taken their own lives! Statistically that is quite high when you think about it! I know their suicides may not have had anything whatsoever to do with the fact that they were mediums, but I do know from experience that mediumistic development can encourage latent psychological problems as well as mediumistic potential. I just wonder what exactly possessed them to do what they did, when they were all quite special people with no apparent problems. From the very beginning of my mediumistic career, I have always desperately needed to know how it all worked and what chemical and electrical processes were apparent when I was actually working mediumistically. I have been connected to an electroencephalograph (EEG) and a biofeedback device and it was clearly apparent that the electrical circuitry of my brain considerably increased while I was conducting a private consultation. Although scientifically it was suggested that these tests did not prove very much in themselves, it did, however, prove to me that my brain activity not only increased, but that I was most definitely in another psychological zone when I was working. Since then I have been subjected to various tests in Hope University, the results of which were never revealed to me. It has always been my opinion that psychic abilities can be scrutinized under laboratory conditions, but mediumistic skills cannot. I was put in a soundproof room and asked to relay information down a telephone to an anonymous individual. This test was referred to as a Ganzfeld-type test without sensory deprivation. As no responses were given to my dialogue, I was left wondering if there was anyone at all at the other end of the line. I thought then as I do now that nothing whatsoever was achieved with the experiments, apart from the actual experience itself. The test was conducted by Dr. Ciarán O'Keeffe, the co-author of my book *The Great Paranormal Clash*. Further experiments were conducted by the National Geographic television channel for a program on criminal profiling. I was given seven maps, and using my pendulum had to pinpoint the exact locations where crimes were committed and where the perpetrators of those crimes actually lived. Although the results were fairly ambiguous, I was told that I had more or less done as well as the geographic profilers who went through the same experiment.

I do believe that with special training psychics could be of immense help to the police in locating the whereabouts of the perpetrators of crimes. I am quite certain that unusual abilities will be an integral part of the science of the future, and psychics will also play an extremely important part in military warfare, perhaps in a time not too far away! Many government agencies are known to employ the services of psychics, and Russia and America allegedly have special units where individuals with psychic abilities are trained.

Chapter Twenty-Four

The Psychology of the New Age!

The so-called 'New Age' has brought an influx of new spiritual concepts based on ancient traditions. The word 'Karma' for example has somehow infiltrated the English language and today seems to be used to suggest that someone should get their comeuppance – payback for the things they have done wrong! Although the word karma is an integral part of the ancient text of many Eastern traditions, it is one of those terms that really became fashionable in the Western world during the 'Flower Power' days of the 1960s, when the devotees of the so-called Hippy Cult preached Love, Peace and Transcendental Meditation. Eastern traditions affirm that karma is in constant operation all through our lives, and that we reap what we sow, not as a punishment for what we have done wrong, but because the effect must always follow the cause. Karma, combined with many other Eastern esoteric words, is today being used as an integral part of New Age terminology, fashionable jargon that culminates into a whole new language, and has somehow today found its way into the vocabulary of Spiritualism. Today the devotees of the paranormal talk about chakras, karma, reincarnation, prana and the aura as though they have their origins in New Age traditions, when these along with many others have formed an important part of Buddhist and Hindu disciplines for thousands of years. Chakras, which literally mean 'wheels' or 'circles' in Sanskrit, are believed to be connected to the endocrine glands and nerve plexuses through an extensive system of channels called 'Nadis'. The word 'nadi' means nerve only at a more subtle level, and it is along these nadis that prana flows from the chakras to the organs of the physical body, maintaining equilibrium and balance. This complex processing of energy has been known to yogic masters for thousands of years and has today somehow evolved into a core of modern teachings propagated by the self-styled gurus of the very fashionable New Age. Prana is the word used to describe all energy in the universe and is the subtle agent through which the life of the body is sustained. The more prana that is drawn into and remains in the body, the higher the quality of life; therefore, a reduction in prana results in the lowering of our vitality and ultimately a deterioration in the quality of our life. Of course, where there is no prana there is no life. Life is solely dependent upon breath, and it is during the process of respiration that prana is drawn into the body. So, we can see that prana has its own particular parts to play in the manifestation of life, apart from the very obvious physiological functions. It's quite interesting that the yogic masters have known about prana for thousands of years, and it is only over the last 20 years or so that science has positively identified 'something' in the air that we breathe that is completely different from oxygen. Prana is the vital force, the manifestation of which is prevalent everywhere. Although the aura has been mentioned elsewhere, for the purpose of this chapter I would like to briefly touch upon it again. The aura is one of those words that the majority of people use without any understanding of its true meaning. Although we frequently hear people say, "This house has an aura of warmth," or "He has an aura of peace about him," the word is far more than a descriptive term. The aura is now a scientific as well as a metaphysical fact, and I suppose is best described as a vaporous mass of electromagnetic particles surrounding every living thing. I have already established that the human aura is the medium through which psychically inclined individuals are able to home in and glean information from the invisible side of the universe. We now know the aura exists because it can be photographed with a special camera in full color. The aura changes with every passing thought and emotion, and glows when we are happy, and is dull when we are sad. Mediums and psychics nearly always refer to it when they are working, and frequently remark on the colors they 'see' in a person's aura. But why are all these esoteric phenomena so important to mediums working today, and 50 years ago or more were veritably unknown? It is quite true to say that 50 to 100 years ago the majority of mediums made no reference to chakras, prana, or for that matter any other of the esoteric words that are so popular today. However, esoteric terminology was known to a select few mediums; and these were in fact privy to a secret core of teachings propagated by an occult organization called the Theosophical Society. Knowledge of subjects that are common-place today were once regarded as 'sacred' and were only given to those who were suitably qualified in a spiritual sense. Of course, the possessors of such knowledge were occasionally willing to prostitute their abilities and pass their knowledge on to the less spiritually equipped, which is why today we have a very eclectic core of teachings, culminating into what has become known as 'New Age'. The psychology behind New Age tradi-tions is really open to interpretation and is solely dependent upon those who pass it on to others. What was once considered extremely precious knowledge has been simplified and is today fashionable and very viable. The power that was once behind these teachings has today long since dissipated into fragments of innumerable different concepts and now bears the hallmark of 'New Age' teachings. What were once frowned upon by Spiritualism and related organizations are today embraced as integral parts of their own teachings. Although many devotees of the New Age treat the whole subject with reverence and respect, a minority approach the teachings lightheartedly and use the various concepts without any real consideration of the spiritual implications. Many of the followers of Pagan traditions also mistakenly use various Eastern concepts, which have over the years become entwined with their own teachings. Even the word

'Kundalini' (the serpent fire) is ignorantly being used by many devotees of both the New Age and Paganism, who talk about its arousal as an essential part of Spiritual Development. Unlike prana, which comes from the sun, kundalini originates from the earth, and lies in the base chakra (Muladhara), looking to all intents and purposes like a sleeping serpent with its mouth closed firmly around the chakra. The belief is that, with the use of certain meditative disciplines, prana is drawn into the base chakra where it causes the serpent to be aroused, at which point it awakens and slowly climbs upwards through the seven major chakras, precipitating each en-route. Although the use of such disciplines to awaken kundalini in this way can be quite dangerous when practiced by the unqualified practitioner, awakening of kundalini does occur quite naturally through the process of spiritual and psychic development. Interest in such matters is clearly evident by the number of books on New Age subjects available on the shelves of every bookseller. Although the majority of people appear to be turning away from traditional religion, there is very little doubt that today there is a spiritual revolution taking place all over the world, and today there is an increase in the amount of people endeavoring to develop their full spiritual and psychic potential.

Chapter Twenty-Five

Anonymity – The Deadly Weapon of the Internet

When I began my career 30 years ago as a professional medium, it never occurred to me for one single moment that there were individuals out there who despised me for what I was doing. It was really only when I began working on the popular television program *Most Haunted* in 2008 that the reality of Internet 'hate' hit me with a vengeance. It was then that I experienced the full wrath of the anonymity of the World Wide Web. Although I did receive hundreds of nice and very complimentary emails, I received a very small number of really hateful ones, obviously designed to offend and hurt me, which of course they did! Had it not been for my wife's support and encouragement, even with all my years of experience, I would have been even more deeply affected! It was then that I realized the power of anonymity and just how much damage an anonymous email can actually do. Although I have since found out that the perpetrator of the majority the 'hate' emails was actually a Liverpool paranormal storyteller (who used different email addresses to hide behind), the reality of just how dangerous these emails can be made me re-assess the part I played in the paranormal. Although there are many people who really approach the subject in a very serious way, there is a small minority who are very unstable and bring the whole subject of the paranormal into disrepute! The subject does sometimes tend to attract a certain kind of very resentful and jealous individuals, someone who delights in sending these very caustic emails, designed primarily to cause maximum hurt. Of course, even when such emails are treated with the contempt they deserve, it is still very frightening to think that there are individuals who are capable of such venom and are willing to use the Internet, blogs and forums to perpetrate such hate. I have already said in an earlier chapter that the paranormal is an emotional minefield, and when you make a detailed analysis of the psychological implications of the paranormal, it is quite easy to see why some of its devotees are unhinged and often psychologically disturbed. Little do the perpetrators of such venomous emails realize what fire they are playing with when they make such wicked attacks. Nor do they fully comprehend that the world of the paranormal operates within the boundaries of certain spiritual laws, and these laws protect those who treat them with respect. Curses and Blessings Come Home to Roost: hate directed anonymously or otherwise at someone who does not deserve it rebounds from its target, returns to the sender and gathers force from the impact! This law is both right and just and is just as effective with hate as it is with love. These laws operate all through our lives and are just as powerfully effective with the hate perpetrated through cyber space as much as they are with physical actions or the spoken word. As well as being an emotional minefield, the paranormal is also a psychological minefield with enormous implications. Becoming involved in the paranormal means empowering it in a way that the naive and the ignorant never dreamed possible. It is very true that a little knowledge is dangerous, especially when that knowledge takes you to the darkest places your mind could ever create. It is here that we are reminded of the ancient precept, "He who rides the tiger's back dare not dismount!" In this case the tiger happens to be the paranormal; once you begin exploring it you can never stop looking! For certain people the paranormal can be extremely dangerous, particularly when some areas of it are touched upon in a frivolous and very careless way. It is certainly not a subject for the nervous or those with a history of psychological problems. You might expect me to advocate getting involved with the paranormal, but you would be completely wrong. Some individuals begin to explore the paranormal and very quickly establish themselves as experts in the field, when they are not. No particular qualifications are required to actually become a serious devotee of the paranormal and run a group. Some so-called 'high profile' parapsychologists are running online courses in parapsychology, and once a medium, parapsychologist or paranormal investigator has appeared frequently on television, he or she is then revered as an expert in the field and then begins to attract their own following of devotees. Unfortunately, regardless of how well-known and well-liked an individual is, when this happens there is always someone who is willing to make a malicious attack on them, usually through an anonymous email. Such individuals do not realize just what dangers they are creating for themselves, and apart from the fact that there is obviously something psychologically wrong with them, they are leading the way through a very dangerous psychological minefield! For many, the paranormal is just one of many ways to make money and increase their bank balance; but others treat the paranormal with a great deal of respect and continue to explore the many areas of the subject quietly and in private.

Chapter Twenty-Six

Can Mediums Really Speak to the Dead?

I have to now lay aside the fact that I am a medium and try my best to analyze the mediumistic process objectively and from a layman's perspective. I have already established that as well as having been a professional medium for nearly 30 years, I am also a skeptic and very suspicious of the majority of mediums in general. There has always been some controversy and question over mediums and the way some demonstrate their alleged skills, but the fact that there are so many mediums today only suffices to cast even more suspicion and doubt on the whole mediumistic profession. It would also seem that the vague and ambiguous information passed on by the majority of mediums is more than likely the reason why an awful lot of people find it very difficult to really believe. Do mediums really receive information from the so-called dead anyway? Are the supporters and followers of mediums at fault, as opposed to the mediums themselves? What is it that genuine mediums are seeing or hearing, and what is it that fake mediums are endeavoring to achieve? If I as a medium find it all very perplexing, what must the general public think? I have for many years tried desperately to understand the psychology behind it all, but the more I have learnt, the less it would seem I know. I am quite sure that fake mediums are not trying to 'fool' the devotees of mediumship as much as they are trying desperately to make money or even to be famous. If the so-called 'dead' are communicating with mediums, where are 'they' communicating from? Does the spirit world really exist? If so, where is it? There are so many questions to be asked, and so many different and very conflicting answers.

If we compare the complex structure of a medium's brain to

the intricate circuitry of a radio receiver, then we are perhaps a little nearer to understanding the whole process. But, a radio receiver will only pick up selected signals that are transmitted from any one of the various radio stations responsible for broadcasting the programs, from anywhere in the world. The listener has to first of all make a choice of which radio station he or she wants to listen to, and then some fine tuning has to be performed in order for the right frequency to be obtained. Mediums (myself included) frequently describe the process of communication in pretty much the same way as the fine-tuning of a radio to pickup the correct frequency. Are we then to suppose that the discarnate communicators are available and ready to communicate all the time or are they only available some times? One can understand why skeptics sometimes have difficulty believing in mediums. Why should they when mediumistic performances are so inconsistent and very unreliable. I have stated so many times in this book that a medium is only as good as the audience he or she is working with.

Stage Craft

On the other hand, an audience can give substance to a stage show and make an inferior medium appear spectacular. The manipulation of an audience is a skill that very few stage mediums possess, and those who do have even a rudimentary form of stage craft know exactly how to control an audience and get the very best from their mediumistic demonstration. Some people are so overwhelmed with the fact that the medium has selected them out of an audience of anything up to 2000 that they find themselves agreeing to everything the medium is saying! Of course, it does not matter to the medium; as long as the recipient's response is positive and the demonstration appears spectacular, that's the most important thing. Occasionally an audience can be extremely impressed with the most ambiguous messages and make the whole performance appear quite astounding. I have never been quite sure whether these sorts of responses are down to lack of education about the way mediums work, or simply the result of shyness from being spoken to in a large auditorium! Whatever the reason, the fact is that the majority of mediums do get away with an awful lot, and who can blame them?

AUDIENCE AWARENESS: I fully understand why a bereaved person would attend a theater demonstration of a so-called well-known medium. After all, that's what mediums are for, isn't it? I do totally understand how a bereaved person must feel when he or she has been taken along to see a medium demonstrate for the very first time. It may even feel as though they are the only one in the theater who has lost someone they love, and so they are certain that they will receive a message from the medium! Although I can understand perfectly why they would feel this way, it is totally the wrong attitude to have. Mediums do have a responsibility to everyone who sits in the audience, regardless of whether or not they have lost someone. However, one must understand the immense pressure that lies on a medium's shoulders when he or she walks onto the stage knowing full well that there is someone in the audience who is absolutely desperate to receive some sort of message from their loved one. The medium is not always at fault here, as some bereaved people should not subject themselves in the first place to a public demonstration, and some should never consult a medium at all! As well as giving a lot of comfort, mediums can also do a lot of emotional damage, particularly if a message is not given in the correct, sensitive way. A question I am always asked is: "What length of time must elapse before a deceased person is able to communicate?" In my experience it is the bereaved person who needs time to recover emotionally. I have known a deceased person to communicate within hours of their passing. It all depends on the circumstances and how spiritually aware a deceased person actually is. It may sound ridiculous, but some people do not want to ever communicate through a medium. Sometimes communication is simply not possible at all, and in fact may never happen. I do think it is quite unfair to cajole someone to consult a medium, regardless of the medium's exemplary reputation. A period of healing must in my opinion always be allowed before even considering consulting a medium. After all, as I have said before, it is an emotional minefield, at least where some people are concerned.

It is often difficult for a bereaved person to understand where their loved one has gone to! Comprehending the nature of death with an understanding of where exactly a person goes when he or she dies is very difficult for the majority of people to fully grasp. It is only when we lose someone we love that our childhood conceptions of heaven and hell are then questioned. Even those who have been indoctrinated into the biblical interpretation of death very often begin to question their belief and what they have been taught when a loss has been suffered. The truth is we can only hypothesize over life after death, and even mediums can only offer their own opinion as to what they believe transpires after death. Nonetheless, we do know that death is not the end, and that life continues after death in one form or another. It was once said to me that when our loved ones die they merely move to a different place in our hearts! Whatever you believe, the fact is the process of communication is not as straightforward as we are led to believe. The so-called 'dead' are not simply energies caught in the ether, living an inactive life until a medium somehow selectively 'homes in' to them; they are very much alive and living on in another surreal dimension. "The dead do not really die!" as nineteenth century dramatist Maurice Maeterlinck once said. "But it is not in your churches they are to be found; but in your thoughts, in your hearts, and in yourselves where they always shall be!" Although Maeterlinck believed totally in mediums and the afterlife, his poetic attempt to beautify the loss of a loved one was perhaps done in such a way as to appeal to those who were not quite ready to look at death from a more profound even scientific perspective. It's all so easy when you do really believe that death is not the end! But actually arriving at that point in your life is perhaps the most difficult thing to embrace. It is extremely difficult to comprehend exactly where the person you have loved for many, many years has gone once his or her last breath has been expelled. It is quite difficult to understand that they are living on in a different place without their family around them. But, the truth is, they are, and will continue to do so until we join them at some time in the future. The psychology of death is more or less the same for everyone; it is emotionally painful and deprives the majority of us of the *will* to carry on! However, most of us get there in the end, and a minority fall at the wayside and simply refuse to continue living without the person they have lost by their side. The most difficult part of life is death, and this is the one thing we all have in common. Even as a medium I have never been too sure that consulting a medium is the best thing to do when you have lost someone you love. Sometimes it can be like rubbing salt into an open wound and can very often prolong the healing process. I have said before, the best and most accurate medium in the world cannot guarantee that he or she will make 'contact' with the person you have lost! I would even go as far as to affirm that the majority of so-called spirit communication is not genuine, and that the best of mediums become proficient psychologists and skilled counsellors. As well as fooling those who consult them, mediums are most of the time fooling themselves. And so, to answer the frequently asked question, "Can mediums really speak to the dead?" I can really only speak for myself; and providing the medium is genuine I must answer: "Yes!" Speaking to the so-called 'dead' is the easy part of the process; the hardest part is hearing what the dead are actually saying to you. And I am quite sure that only a small minority of mediums can actually hear anything at all!

Terminology and Things You Should Know

As I have already affirmed, today the paranormal has become hugely fashionable and has given rise to a whole new language – terminology with which only the devotees of the paranormal can be privy. I suppose it is only fair to give credit where credit is due and the innumerable paranormal television programs are today essentially responsible for giving birth to a whole new fashion of ghosts, haunted houses and all things paranormal. Of course, the paranormal must be considered an umbrella term and covers a very broad spectrum of topics, from the common-place creaks, knocks and bumps of an alleged haunted location, to the analytical views of the parapsychologist. Orbs, residual, visitation, astral beings, light anomaly and EMF meter are just some of the frequently over exploited terms that are used on ghost hunting programs and which have given new meanings to some everyday words. There has also been an increase in the sales of so-called 'ghost hunting' equipment such as EMF meters, non-contact infrared thermometers, night vision cameras and many other sophisticated paranormal devices, essential equipment for every self-respecting Ghost Hunter or Paranormal Investigator. Parapsychology, the hundred-year-old pseudo-science, has also set the trend for those interested in the inves-tigative scientific side of the paranormal, by popularizing a wide range of scientific gadgets and even more parapsychological terms to explain the various paranormal phenomena. It would appear that some parapsychologists are not exempt from exploiting the paranormal's commercial bandwagon, with the announcement, "You too can be a parapsychologist by enrolling on an online course!" It is all now very viable, and whichever way you choose to embark upon the great paranormal adventure, you can be certain that there will always be those prepared to pay the suggested fee, regardless of how much that is! Let's explore some of the terminology used by paranormal investigators, along with the terms used by parapsychologists to define some psychological phenomena.

APOPHENIA: A term coined by Klaus Conrad, primarily to describe the psychological phenomenon of seeing patterns or connections in random or meaningless abnormal data.

PAREIDOLIA: Finding images or sounds in random stimuli. The best example of Pareidolia is when you think the phone is ringing or perhaps that someone has called your name while you are taking a shower.

IDEOMOTOR ACTION/EFFECT: Refers to the influence of suggestions or expectation on involuntary and unconscious motor behavior. Term created by William Benjamin Carpenter 1852 to explain why the pointer moves on a Ouija board.

THE BARNUM EFFECT: A term coined by psychologist Paul Meehl in reference to the great circus man, Phineas Taylor Barnum, a psychological manipulator who always proclaimed, "We have something for everyone!" The term is now used to describe subjective validation in which an individual finds personal meaning in general and ambiguous statements given by mediums that could apply to anyone.

ESP – EXTRASENSORY PERCEPTION: Popularized by Joseph Banks Rhine, Duke University 1927.

ANALYTICAL AND ASSOCIATIVE OVERLAY: Psychic impressions resulting in extraneous impressions and images being commingled with psychic ones.

THE FORER EFFECT: Named after Bertram R. Forer and refers to the tendency of people to rate sets of statements as highly accurate for them personally even though the statements could apply to many people.

ORBS: Light anomalies usually caught either on films or photographs.

EMF METER: Electromagnetic fluctuation meter. A small device that measures fluctuations in the electromagnetic range or atmosphere.

NON-CONTACT LASER THERMOMETER: A hand-held

device with a laser beam to monitor the temperature in the far side of a room.

TRIBOLUMINESCENCE: A geological phenomenon produced by the friction of crystals or other minerals below ground level.

BIOLUMINESCENCE: An optical phenomenon sometimes seen in some aquatic creatures, and is produced by chemical energy converted into light energy by the cells of the body, before culminating into the bioluminescence, a luminous glow around the entire body.

THE HUMAN AURA: The human organism is an electromagnetic unit of incredible power, assimilating, processing and discharging energy, and is contained within its own spectrum of light and color. The aura is probably best described as a vaporous mass of electromagnetic energy surrounding all living things.

THE STONE TAPE THEORY: A paranormal hypothesis speculating that inanimate matter is able to absorb human energy during highly tense moments, such as murder or intense moments of human life. The hypothesis, created some time in the 1970s, suggests that the bricks and mortar of a building store images and sounds in the same way that images and sounds are captured on video or audio tapes. The speculation is that ghosts are not really the manifestation of spirits, but phenomena produced by the 'stone tape' theory, subtle energy recordings.

KIRLIAN CAMERA: A crude photographic device invented by husband and wife team Semyon and Valentina Kirlian from Krasnodar near the Black Sea. Their invention produced monochrome images of the radiations of energy emanating from the hands, and served as a diagnostic tool and an inspiration to others working in the same field. The Kirlians believed that all disease was visible in the aura some considerable time before it became apparent in the body.

KILNER AURA SCREENS: Medical electronics expert Walter

Kilner, radiologist from St Thomas' Hospital, London, developed a simple way of allowing the aura to be seen by even the non-psychically inclined person. A special coal tar dye (dicyanin) was poured between two glass screens. When the patient stood in front of the screens with a bright light behind them, his or her aura became visible. Kilner published his studies of the aura in his bestselling book, *The Human Atmosphere*, later renamed *The Aura*.

CLAIRVOYANCE: The ability to 'see' things that the normal person cannot! A mediumistically inclined person possesses the ability to 'see' so-called 'dead' people.

CLAIRAUDIENCE: This is the ability to 'hear' supersensual sounds, such as disembodied voices.

CLAIRSENTIENCE: Loosely defined as 'clear sensing', clairsentience is usually described as our prehistoric 'homing' device, and is the one thing we all share in common.

CHANNELLING: The process of conveying information while in a semi or even deep trance-like state. However, some individuals who practice channeling remain fully conscious during the whole process, and yet appear 'uplifted' or in a state of euphoria!

TRANCE MEDIUMSHIP: This is a medium through whom a disembodied voice speaks while they appear to be in a light sleep. Some trance mediums have the ability to change from one state of consciousness to another with no apparent effort.

HYPNAGOGIC: The psychological state to describe the consciousness before the onset of sleep, during which one sometimes experiences visual and auditory phenomena.

HYPNOPOMPIC: The states of sensory awareness experienced as we wake up, sometimes accompanied by visual and auditory phenomena.

CRYSTAL SPECULUM: Reflective surface or crystal ball favored by seers and fortunetellers of old; a tool of divination to glean information about the future.

PENDULUM: A small object (crystal or wooden shape) attached to a length of string or chain for purpose of dowsing.

OUIJA BOARD: Originally sold as a toy to communicate with spirits. The Ouija Board consists of letters of the alphabet and the words 'yes' and 'no'. The user places their finger lightly on a wooden pointer, which moves of its own accord from letter to letter, spelling out a message. When a question requiring a simple 'yes' or 'no' is asked, the pointer responds.

DOWSING RODS: Two L shaped rods used to dowse for water or energy fields. The user holds one in each hand, and when the source has been located the rods begin to move.

PLANCHETTE: A small writing device housing a pencil, used primarily to receive writing from a disembodied person.

SÉANCE TRUMPET: This is an elongated cone-shaped trumpet, usually made of aluminum, with a luminous strip allowing it to be seen through the total darkness of a séance room. When the séance phenomena have been successfully achieved, the levitating trumpet resounds with a disembodied voice, stopping at a seemingly carefully selected member of the séance.

CHAKRA: Literally meaning 'Wheel' or 'Circle' in Sanskrit, are spiritual energy centers strategically located across the surface of the spinal column, and are believed to be connected to the endocrine glands and nerve plexuses through an extensive system of channels called nadis (mentioned below).

NADI: The word nadi literally means 'nerve' only at a more subtle level. Pranic energy (mentioned below) is conveyed along the nadis, from the chakras to the organs of the physical body, maintaining health and balance.

PRANA: Prana is the vital force, and is the name used in esoteric teachings to describe ALL energy in the universe. Prana is the subtle agent through which the life of the body is sustained. It can be controlled by a yogic system of breathing called 'Pranayama'.

TABLE TIPPING: The Victorian séance phenomenon allegedly produced by discarnate energies. The individuals seated around the heavy table place their hands on the shiny surface, and if successful the table will either rock from side to side, or lift from the floor without the help of those involved in the practice.

SÉANCE: A method of communicating with the so-called 'dead', favored by Victorian Spiritualists.

SPIRITUALISM: A religion based on the belief that communication can be made with disembodied souls through a medium.

SCRYING: Fixing the gaze on one particular point of an object, usually as a means of focusing the attention.

YANTRA: Geometric shape or design used in Eastern meditation practices.

MANDALA: Geometric shape used in Buddhist meditation.

MANTRA: Often considered a 'power' word and chanted as a discipline during meditation.

PINEAL GLAND: One of the endocrine glands that secrets melatonin into the bloodstream and is situated beneath the back part corpus callosum. The pineal is believed to be responsible for the production of psychic skills.

ALPHA: Oscillating electrical voltages in the brain usually produced during deep meditation.

MEDITATION: One of many mental disciplines used primarily to focus and make the mind quiet. Meditation is an ancient system of mental disciplines with which to focus the attention on one thing to the exclusion of all else.

PSYCHIC DEVELOPMENT: The term used to describe the process of cultivating the faculties with the sole intention of heightening the awareness.

KUNDALINI: An energy located in the chakra at the base of the spine. Sometimes referred to as the 'Serpent Fire' primarily because of its potency, but in some Yogic circles it is known as Prana Shakti. There are specific meditation exercises to activate kundalini, usually practiced under the supervision of an experienced practitioner or teacher.

I have only listed some of the terms I think would be useful to anyone making a study of the paranormal and esoteric matters. To confuse matters even more, there are three times as many terms as there are mediums, psychics and paranormal groups. This book was intended to enlighten you as to the reality of the paranormal and mediums, and not simply to educate those who are already convinced!

Concluding Observations

The one single thing we all have in common is death! We are all going to die. As yet nobody has quite found a way around that, so I think we can safely assume at the moment that death is unavoidable. Unless of course you are fortunate to perceive death as the beginning of a new life; then you most probably believe that when your physical body dies some spiritual part of you will continue to live on in some other more refined dimension, popularly referred to as the *Spirit World*. For those who do not believe that there is anything beyond death, then I'm afraid that complete annihilation is inevitable! Well, that's what you expect, isn't it? As a medium it is quite easy for me to believe in an afterlife. In fact, belief in an afterlife is a prerequisite for my work as a medium. My job would be pretty pointless otherwise, don't you think? After all, it is a medium's job to prove to the bereaved that life continues beyond death by giving personal information from their deceased relatives that nobody else but they could possibly have known. But could the concept of an afterlife just be something that our prehistoric forbears created out of their fear of death? Or, could there be something else going on that we don't really know about, but most people inwardly suspect? Do the majority of those who affirm that they totally believe in an afterlife really believe, or are they simply deluding themselves because of the inherent fear they themselves have of death? As I have already said in a previous chapter, even those who rubbish the very suggestion of an afterlife nearly always have a story to tell about one experience or another. Whenever I am giving a talk, or even demonstrating my mediumistic skills in a theater, there is always a skeptic there at the conclusion of the event to let me know what he or she thinks. "You don't believe in all that stuff do you?" they always smugly grin. "Mediums can't talk to the dead! The dead are dead!" Yeah, right! But then, once they engaged me in conversation, without fail they always add, "It is all rubbish; but there was this one time when... " I think I am safe in saying that the majority of people have had an unexplainable 'spooky' experience at sometime in their lives, even though they very often don't directly relate it to the paranormal. So you can probably see why I do not believe that there is such an entity as a skeptic!

I do believe that the way we perceive the paranormal and life beyond death very often depends entirely on how we were brought up by our parents. Not only do we understandably genetically inherit a great deal of our mental capacity from our parents, but what our parents have inherited from their parents very often makes them program us from a very early age to think in a certain way. It is perhaps only a small minority who develop the ability to break away, so to speak, from this parental programming, to become something other than what their parents wanted them to be. In saying this there has to be a force other than parental programming in operation in some families. What makes a child grow up devoutly religious in an atheistic family, desperately wanting to devote his or her life to the church? Coincidence? I think not! Genetic memory? Possibly. Providing someone in the family archives had similar religious intentions. Try as they may, parapsychologists know as much about the psychology of genuine mediumship as the majority of mediums know about the way their own abilities actually work. I have no doubt whatsoever that there are psychological implications to the paranormal, and that those who naively get involved in it are entering a psychological minefield.

Anecdotal accounts of other people's paranormal experiences I do believe are totally unreliable, as the majority of people tend to embellish their experience to make it more credible and interesting. However, by the time the individual's experience has been passed around, in the tradition of Chinese Whispers, the whole thing becomes something else. I have seen this so many times when people have come to see me at my office. The story they have told me was not the story that was first brought to my attention by, of course, somebody else.

Skeptics though are a different breed, and really do live in a different universe to even parapsychologists. Even seeing is not always believing to the skeptic, who will always disagree just for the sake of an argument. And even the person with a genuine paranormal experience to relate is very often cajoled into doubting what they really experienced. I always use the analogy of the white crow. Because we have only ever seen black crows, the man who saw a white crow was ridiculed to such an extent that he eventually began to doubt that he had seen a white crow, and eventually changed his mind.

Those who consult mediums and the like have to trust that what he or she is saying is true; but it tends to be human nature to only believe what pleases us and to reject what doesn't make sense, even though what doesn't make sense may well be true.

6th Books investigates the paranormal, supernatural, explainable or unexplainable. Titles cover everything included within parapsychology: how to, lifestyles, beliefs, myths, theories and memoir.